MW01166925

THE INth DEGREE

HOW TO STAND OUT
BY GOING *All* IN

TIFFANY MCQUAID
WITH BRUCE LITTLEFIELD

ISBN 979-8-9892176-9-4

TO MY MOM & DAD IN HEAVEN,
THANK YOU FOR ALL YOUR LOVE AND LESSONS

TABLE OF CONTENTS

TABLE OF CONTENTS

INTRODUCTION

WE'RE GOING ALL IN.

IT'S THE ONLY WAY TO STAND OUT!

You may be one of the 31 million entrepreneurs running a business in the United States alone or one of the 543,000 getting ready to start one today. You could be a salesperson selling gadgets or a landscaper providing a service. You might just be starting your career and received this book as a graduation present. No matter what your business card or diploma says, you need to know something. You're in the business of offering. What are you offering? A better future. A better future for both the person who buys what you're selling and for yourself in selling it.

What's out of your control? The past. Other people's behavior. And the weather. The things IN your control? Your attitude. Your words. Your creativity. The boundaries you set. What you look at, take in, consume. And, most of all, your determination to make things happen. Working towards a dream is exciting, scary, and often like walking a tightrope without a safety net.

So, let's start by stopping. Stop thinking, stop worrying, stop strategizing what others want from us and instead concentrate first on what we want from ourselves. Good old Socrates told us, "To know thyself is the beginning of wisdom." It's also what's going to make you authentically irresistible so that you attract great things to your life and business like iron to a magnet.

You might be feeling lost right now. You know there is more, but how do you get there? You might be worried about how you're going to pay the pile of outstanding invoices on your desk, feeling hopeless about keeping your staff, or wondering why your business is stagnant, and why customers aren't flocking in. You might be an entrepreneur about to start a new venture or thinking about giving up on the one you've been working at for years. You might be a salesperson who is just hoping for your next big deal. You want to go further, but how do you do that without losing your energy, your patience, your kindness, and your shirt?!

The last few years have been rather difficult in this world of ours. From politics to pandemic, we've all gone through some things. We're tired. Exhausted, really. You might be realizing that you can't continue down the same path, doing the same things. You may even feel like you want to give up — on everything. I've been there, too, but as I'm going to share with you, I found that it's in those moments — the ones in which you feel that there's no way forward — that real growth happens. Those moments, when we think we've already done everything we can, present the opportunity to make magic materialize.

Life and business are filled with ups and downs, and I'm going to share some of mine with you — the good, the bad, the over-the-top as we go all IN to take our lives and business to the next level, to The INth degree.

SO, WHO AM I AND WHY ARE YOU TAKING ADVICE FROM ME?

Since this is an introduction, let me introduce myself.

Originally from Ohio, I'm now President of McQuaid & Company, an innovative real estate firm in Naples, Florida, that I founded in 2013 when I recognized a market opportunity and took a running leap. My business makes millions of dollars a year because I (and the company I keep) have an INth Degree vision of who we are and where we want to go. I've found people are attracted to that. My firm is special because we do things with focus, take creative (and sometimes extreme) risks to stand out, and invite others to join our party. I've handpicked each member of my team because they are dynamic go-getters who sprinkle a little joy wherever they go. Our motto is: "If we can believe in something great, we can achieve something great."

I sell houses for a living, but you might be selling widgets, running a doctor's office, managing an auto body shop, or setting up a housewares store. It's not what we're selling. It's who is doing the selling and how. That translated is... how does your energy and presentation make others feel? An enlightened entrepreneur knows the value is IN you.

The INth Degree is the indispensable system I created and use to find myself, know myself, and differentiate myself in the world. My business has become successful as a result. Its Seven Keys are:

INTREPIDNESS Resolute fearlessness, fortitude, and endurance. *It's the daring ability to keep going.*

INVIGORATION The act of giving vitality to make oneself feel healthier, spunkier, more energetic. *It's what makes a day exciting.*

INTENTION An aim, a plan, a goal, a determination to operate a certain way. *It's the purpose.*

INSPIRATION The mental stimulation to do, to feel, to create, and to take action. *It's the why. Period.*

INGENUITY The quality of being clever, original, and inventive. *It's the problem-solving miracle.*

INCENTIVE What motivates or encourages one to do something. *It's what makes all of us tick.*

INFLUENCE To have an effect on the behavior of someone. *When it's joyful, it's a superpower.*

So, here's the question:

WHAT DO YOU WANT TO BRING INTO YOUR LIFE?

Take a moment and visualize it. Is it emotional, spiritual, physical, romantic, financial, or something completely different? Whatever that is, there is only one person who can deliver that. The person who can change your life, find the solution to your problems, and make you happy. Who is that? Look in the mirror.

IT'S YOU.

I'm not trying to walk you on the path to becoming a quote-loving, red-dress wearing, big smile smiling, unabashed cheerleader. That's me. We're looking for you! We're looking to bring out authentic, bold, excited, big success YOU. What I know is that INcremental steps lead to victory. (See what I did there?!) My hope is that as I share my stories and these Seven Keys, you'll be inspired to find the best version of yourself. What you'll see in mine is that even though I've had my share of life's punches, which I'll tell you about, I've come out of it remaining my glass-is-*full* self.

I've unlocked a lot of doors in my day, but the door I'd like to help you unlock opens to your INth Degree — that's all the goodness inside you, the goodness that will help you realize the best version of yourself, and the goodness you can give to and get from this world.

This book is a manifesto on believing in your capabilities, getting clever, and achieving great satisfaction and happiness in your life by going all IN with hope, joy and kindheartedness. The gift with purchase is super success in your business.

LET'S UNLOCK THAT DOOR.

INTREPIDNESS

KEY 1

THE QUALITY OF MIND ENABLING ONE TO FACE HARDSHIP RESOLUTELY: BRAVERY, COURAGE, FEARLESSNESS, FORTITUDE, METTLE, NERVE, PLUCK, SPIRIT, SPUNK.

IT'S THE DARING ABILITY TO KEEP GOING!

I'm going to start by getting the really awful out of the way. I need to share a paralyzing family secret. A family secret that everyone knew, but no one could talk about. The kind of secret that, when it happened, no one would ever share with ten-year-old me. This was both life-altering and suffocating because I knew the secret, but no one knew that I did.

Up until the day it had happened, I had had a relatively pleasant childhood. My hometown of Suffield, Ohio, fifteen or so miles southeast of Akron, was pretty ordinary. Many of the residents, including my dad, headed for work into Akron, the "Rubber Capital of the World," where both The Goodyear Tire & Rubber Company and Firestone were based.

My dad David was a brilliant man, a self-taught chemist, who worked for many years at Firestone. He was super funny, always making people laugh and smile, and certainly loved by all. Thinking back on it, he was also a chameleon. He rarely looked the same. His tall, slender frame being the only constant. The "norm" was his dark brown hair perfectly straight with a feathered swoop at top, but then he'd randomly get a perm and sport an Afro for a while. Sometimes he'd cut that short, so the curls would just give it body. Occasionally, he would have a full beard. Other times, just a mustache, sometimes nothing. I now recognize his changing appearance might have been indicative of internal conflict and struggle.

My mom and dad shared similarly challenging childhoods. My dad bounced between the four houses of my grandmother's sisters during the week and then spent weekends with his mother. His dad was an alcoholic, and his parents divorced at a time when that was uncommon. My mom was in numerous foster homes growing up because her mother was a lounge singer and traveled a lot. Shared hardships were connection points in my parents' relationship, and their marriage got them both out of troubling situations. They were together for 13 or so years before my dad's destructive habits started to cause marital problems. Though my mother never shared details with my sister and me or spoke ill of him once, I am confident there were numerous things she could have said.

By the time I was eight or nine years old, I could sense that things were not good between them. They were fighting a lot. Once during a heated argument, I snuck out of my room to peek at them from the hallway. I witnessed my dad slap my mother across the face and she fell backward. I raced into the living room to stop him, and he took off out the front door.

When I was nine years old, my grandmother (my mom's mother) took me on a trip to a lake in Canada. It was a great trip. There was an outhouse, a new oldfangled thing for me, and I got to fish. Even though I don't eat fish, I've always loved fishing. I fished using bologna and hot dogs as bait because I didn't want to hurt the worms. (Don't tell the pig!) We also went to a general store where my grandmother bought a set of "Day of the Week" underwear for me (in case I lost track), and I used my own money to buy my dad a jar of candy-coated peanuts and my mom a jar of gumdrops. It was a sweet weekend that ended in bitter sadness. When my grandmother brought me home, both of my parents were there. I excitedly gave them their treats, and they gave me the news that they were separating, and my dad was moving out. To this day, I can still feel the gut-piercing stab I felt in that moment. It was the first time I ever felt the sorrow of heartache.

My dad relocated to a rental house which I remember as dark and eerily cold. The walls were mint green, and the baseboards were glossy mint green. It wasn't what I'd describe as minty fresh, more minty tragic. Cat Stevens' "Morning Has Broken" played on repeat and became the soundtrack of our visits. Brach's Chocolate Covered Nuts were always in a bowl on his mint green Formica kitchen counter.

Visitation was every other weekend and even though I wanted to see my dad, I didn't like going there. My dad knew we were uncomfortable there and, on his weekends with us, he started taking us to his mother's house. Even though I only went to his rental a few times, I vividly remember its weird feeling and its creepy vibe. Maybe I sensed something bad would happen there.

It was 1980, and the tire industry was changing. Firestone started requiring its scientists to have college degrees, which my dad did not have. Even though he had been working as a chemist for years, he was being forced to go to college to keep his job. He didn't want to, but, out of necessity, he enrolled at Akron University, resentfully paying his $100 deposit.

My dad had my sister and me the weekend after Thanksgiving that year, and we were once again staying at his mother's house. When he announced we were going shopping, we got so excited. It was the beginning of the holiday season and trees and lights were already proclaiming the coming festivities.

Our local shopping center, Chapel Hill Mall, had an unusual oddity that I loved growing up. Archie — a giant talking snowman — was a fixture in the décor. We wanted to see Archie as much as Santa. Kids used a microphone to talk to Archie. When he spoke, his eyes lit up. An often-told family story was Archie asking me what I wanted for Christmas. My seven-year-old response had been, "I want some office supplies. You know, the usual

"Sadness is but a wall between two gardens."

Khalil Gibran

3

— paper clips, but colored ones not the silver kind, a stapler, an ink pad with a stamper, and some pens." The line behind us laughed. Everyone else wanted a Barbie or Baby Alive, but I wanted office supplies. Could Archie see an entrepreneur in my future?

INQUIRY: What's the most memorable present you've ever received?

For this visit, we made our first stop to see Archie, but then my dad revealed he was taking us to JCPenney, a two-level merchandise extravaganza. They had everything, and he said we could pick something out for ourselves. The exhilaration of finding the perfect item was both exciting and engrossing. I took the quest seriously. I wanted to pick just the right thing, something that would bring me hours of enjoyment. While my sister looked at the Strawberry Shortcake ragdolls and the "Rubik's Cube," I was diving into the craft section.

I've always been into art projects and doodling. My school notebooks were filled with colorful squiggles, and at JCPenney, I hit the pot of gold! There were packets of colored pencils, the kind you pull the tip out and push it in the end, so a sharp new piece pops out. There were 20 pencils in a rainbow of glitter colors. I couldn't wait to get home and start using them all! I remember being thrilled by my perfect find. I wanted them so badly and could see myself as the most colorful note writer at Suffield Elementary!

My dad had other ideas.

When I took him my multi-colored treasure, he said, "No, no, no. I want you to get this." He handed me a 45 record.

"I really want the pencils," I said desperately.

"No, Tiffany," he said. "I want you to have this record, and when you go home, I want you to play it for your mom." He knew Santa had given me a record player the year before. "You're going to want more records for your stereo, anyway," he said. "So, you can add this to your collection. Just make sure you play it for your mom."

I didn't know that not only was I not getting my dream gift, but I was also becoming my dad's pawn and used for his personal agenda.

When we returned to my mom's house that weekend, I dutifully called my mom into my bedroom. "Dad wanted me to play this for you," I said, unaware of the heavy significance. I lifted the arm of my little record player and placed the needle onto the spinning black disc.

"Babe I'm leaving... I must be on my way..." the song began playing. "Babe" by Styx was a number-one single in 1979, and tells the story of two people separating.

By the second chorus, "Babe, I'm leaving. I'll say it once again, and somehow try to smile..." my mother had heard enough. She lifted the needle and Styx scratched to silence.

As she walked out of my room, I longed for the glittery pencils.

Two weekends later, my sister and I were back at my grandmother's house with my dad. He seemed different, noticeably not quite himself. He did something, though, that quickly erased the weirdness from my thoughts. He took us to Toys "R" Us and told us to pick out whatever we wanted. Unlike the record experience, this was the best shopping trip in my ten years. My sister picked out a Barbie Dream House. I got a shiny, red Schwinn Varsity Sport 10-speed. Dad even let my cousin, who was with us, pick something. It was like I'd won a gameshow! A capital "S" Splurge! When we marched into my grandmother's house with our new gifts, she freaked out at the excess. "David!" my grandmother exclaimed. "Why would you spend hundreds of dollars on the girls so close to Christmas?"

Two weeks later, on Christmas morning, we would get our answer.

We went to my Aunt Trudy's house for our early Christmas dinner, and I'll never forget the knock on the door. You don't want police to knock on the front door, especially on Christmas.

My mother stepped out onto Aunt Trudy's front porch. After speaking in low mumbles, she came inside, closed the door, and collapsed in the corner of the

"The marks humans leave are too often scars."

John Green
The Fault in Our Stars

dining room, which was beautifully set for the Christmas dinner we wouldn't have. Our mother's face was bloodless, as frosty white as Christmas snow. They awkwardly pulled her up and supported her trembling body against the dining room wall.

The trio cumbersomely went to my Aunt Trudy's bedroom and closed the door. I looked at my sister, and my sister looked back at me. Since she's five years younger, I didn't know if she knew how bad it seemed.

My grandmother eventually came to get my sister and me, saying that mom wanted to talk to us. We warily went into Aunt Trudy's room where our mother was sitting on the floor. We all sat in a circle on the rug, and she grabbed our hands. "Your dad," she said, her voice quavering. "Your dad... has passed away."

"Passed away?" I asked.

"Your dad died," she explained. "He was sick. He was not well. He passed away because of it. But we'll be okay together. I promise."

I was young. How do you process death, the death of your father, when you are only ten years old? That was just the beginning of the damaging Christmas gift my father left.

The following day, I was in the one bathroom in our house, which was adjacent to my mother's bedroom. I overheard my mom talking to her friend on the phone. Through tears, she described my dad's death. "He committed suicide using Cyanide that he had taken from the lab," she said. "He left some for me in an envelope and told me that if I truly loved him, I would take it so I could join him." He also reminded her to get back the hundred dollars he'd left as a deposit at Akron University.

It is very difficult for a young girl to know that her dad "chose" to leave Earth. I didn't dare tell my mother I knew what he'd done for fear she would be mad at me. I kept it to myself, harboring his and her secret. It was a heavy weight to carry and no one to turn to for help, not even a hug. We were a family of non-hugging Catholics. In time, we found there was little to no comfort, and worse, our extended family believed that when someone commits suicide, they go to Hell. Nobody wanted to talk about my dad. It was like he never existed, as though the association would also doom them to Hell. Quietly, my mother, sister, and I were, for the most part, ostracized from our extended family. The saving grace was my dad's mother and his sister, Aunt Bev. Both stepped up to show us love in my dad's absence.

"Trauma is a fact of life. It does not, however, have to be a life sentence."

Peter A. Levine

My dad's death quietly ate at me. The secret was paralyzing, leaving me feeling not just alone, but anxious, ashamed, and confused. I took his death personally, thinking there was something I could have done to keep him here. I always wondered. I lived with a constant fear that my mom would do as the letter said and follow his lead.

He left my mother a diamond heart necklace and one for my sister and me, too. I lost it. Perhaps it was an accident or more likely purposeful as it was too painful a souvenir. After college, I finally told my mother that I knew he committed suicide. She shared a copy of his suicide note that the police had given her.

Years later, I ripped it into pieces.

Why have I shared this painful story with you? To show that no one's life is all sunshine and rainbows. Even the eternal optimist (me!) must, at times, cope with hopelessness. We all encounter hardships and adversities on our journey. These can either destroy us or propel us to our better selves.

Intrepidness is the courage to push forward, carry on, even when the darkness overwhelms us. Sometimes, we simply must find a way to put one foot in front of the other.

For ten-year-old me, that was literal. I had been dancing since I was two and after my dad's death, I went all in. Dance, and my dance teacher Pat, lit a light in my darkness, took me out of my sorrow, and gave comfort to my discomfort. She offered me hope for a better day. Pat's motivation helped me push past the pain of my loss and feel the passion of my present. Dance became nourishment for my starving soul.

Pat was incredibly creative, had an innovative vision, and always expected more and more from us. She took notice of my potential and my drive to learn. Her encouragement synced with my life, giving me a happy spark, and a goal. Working towards something with my dance troupe was a perfect metaphor for life and provided a path to healing. My troupe became very tight and began to compete nationally, winning many competitions. There's one ritual that, to this day, I think of and feel its power. Before we'd go on stage, we would all gather in a circle, connect our pinkies, and say, "Let's go, girls!" Sometimes the smallest things can take up the biggest room in our hearts and minds. Game flipping on! Through these experiences, I learned to handle wins with kinetic energy, loss with grace, and to boldly never stop trying.

Dance enabled me to deal with my personal tragedy, and Pat's motivation helped me realize that a negative mind does not cultivate a positive life. **When we're down, we must seek what pulls us up.** In doing so, with intrepidness, our spirit grows. We just have to keep on moving.

Insight on INTREPIDNESS

You might suspect that Christmas Day is hard for me. You'll substantiate that suspicion when I tell you that decades after my father's death, I also found out — on Christmas Day — that my (now) ex-Lou was cheating on me. That was a blow, especially since we also got engaged on Christmas Day many years prior. When I didn't unwrap anything from Victoria's Secret, (after having seen a lot of purchases on our American Express bill), I figured out the unsolved mystery and proved it by sleuthing through his cell phone bill. There, I saw the hundreds of calls he'd had with my housekeeper. The confrontation proved my gumshoe fears were valid. He wasn't calling her to talk about the dust on the credenza. This wrecked me with wounds more excruciating than anything that bleeds. Once again, I had to climb out of it by being resolute that life was going to deal me a better hand.

Today, I make the best of the Christmas holiday by finding joy in making others smile. I don't put up a tree at home, but I go all in on creatively unleashing my inner elf at our office. Each year, I create a unique theme and come in early to spend five or so hours making Christmas magic. I can't wait for my team to see what insane vision I crafted. Although festive, no one would call it traditional.

As things happen, the Christmas gift of finding out Lou was having an affair couldn't have come at a worse time. I was just starting my own brokerage. By all accounts, I should never have made it beyond the first year. I started my business with $17,000 cash on hand. Although I had a very successful real estate career, the devastating hemorrhage of my 14-year relationship took its toll on my heart and on my finances.

To stay in my home and community, which was my "home base" and biggest source of referrals for my real estate practice, I had to

> "Inaction breeds doubt and fear. Action breeds confidence and courage. If you want to conquer fear, do not sit home and think about it. Go out and get busy."
>
> Dale Carnegie

quickly come up with the money to buy Lou out of his half of the house. To do that, I liquidated all my savings. Not only that, my business manager, marketing director, and assistant, all wanted to join my new firm. I couldn't leave them behind. So, on top of rent and general start-up expenses, I had their salaries. Looking back on it, I cringe at how daring I was. Can you imagine the gamble?

There have been at least four times since opening my own business that I thought I would be forced to close my doors — major market fluctuations, a pandemic, and two devastating hurricanes. Unlike a corporation or franchise, I have no one to lean on in difficult times. I kept my boots on the ground selling and poured my commissions back into the company to cover expenses. I only pulled out what I needed for my personal bare-bone basics.

These times were the most challenging in my life. I elected to eat cereal for dinner during these difficulties to ensure my core team was paid and the lights stayed on. I called these periods my "cereal moments." The sacrifice was real and my feelings were intense. The fear I felt every day knowing that I did not have a cushion or someone to catch me if I fell was daunting. Between selling and managing the company, I was working around the clock to keep it all going. This stress-plus-fear concoction was a dangerous potion to both my physical and mental health. I kept focusing on the end goal because failure was simply not an option.

It was difficult watching those I worked alongside (and was struggling to pay) take fun vacations. I desperately needed an escape, but my only travel was to industry conferences where I was speaking or attending to learn and keep us out ahead of the competition. It was a double-edged sword. On one hand I was glad I was able to provide for them as they worked so hard for me, but on the other, I felt some resentment that I was working in overdrive to ensure that everyone had what they needed, except myself.

Once, when covering payroll was going to be impossible, I decided to part with a special, sentimental gift. My ex-Lou had given me a Rolex watch for my 40th birthday. My heart was already broken from the split and the fact it was the last thing I was holding onto in terms of connectivity made it even more painful. Knowing its value, I asked my assistant, Helen, to sell it. I couldn't bring myself to broker the deal, so off Helen went. She came back an hour later with enough cash to cover that period's payroll, allowing me to exhale for two weeks.

Yes, I've heard business gurus say, "You must always pay yourself first." Sometimes that's easier said than done! I can vividly recall driving home one day listening to a podcast and hearing that paying yourself first is a steadfast Entrepreneurship 101 rule. "Oh, sure!" I said aloud. "How do you do that when you are barely scraping by?"

I had to recalibrate to learn that lesson. I eventually realized that by not paying myself, even a pittance of a paycheck, I had closed the door to receiving. I was making hundreds of thousands of dollars in commissions but was never seeing it. Instead of allowing more abundance to flow in, I had mentally put the cap on the well. Experience is a tough teacher. It gives you the pop quiz first and the lesson comes after. "Cereal moments" aren't healthy in any way. I changed course and began reinvesting 90% of my commissions and keeping 10% for myself. It was the least I could do.

Recently, I walked out to a parking lot in a development I was showing and noticed all these clovers growing through the pavement. What a feat! These delicate, yet mighty, little leaves reaching for the sky. It reminded me that

"Don't worry about the world coming to an end today. It is already tomorrow in Australia."

Charles M. Schulz

determination and optimism can penetrate any and every obstacle when you can continue to believe in your mission and channel your tenacity. It also reminded me of my grandmother assigning us quadrants in her yard and telling us to search for four leaf clovers. While we were on the hunt for good fortune, she said we could also pick all the pretty yellow flowers, which I now know to be dandelions. Driven by the optimistic encounter of a four-leaf find, she skillfully got us to weed her yard.

Looking for good luck is how I've always gotten through tough times. Yes, perhaps naivety is one of my best assets. Like that clover pushing through concrete, I've been able to push through unchartered territories even when there's been fear of the unknown. As I've built my business, intrepid determination has become my battle cry. It's gotten me through when I've been sucker punched by reality. I've internally named myself the Real Estate Rocky, and I enter the ring every day without boxing gloves.

"I've learned that you can tell a lot about a person by the way he handles these three things: a rainy day, lost luggage, and tangled Christmas tree lights."

Maya Angelou

Every entrepreneur needs champion-level intrepidness — to dare to start something from nothing, to be determined enough to ignore naysayers and the doubting demons of your own mind that say you're not good enough, strong enough, or smart enough. It takes pluck to remain flexible, to be willing to pivot, and to continually bet on oneself, even when the last bet wasn't a winner.

There will be setbacks. Consider those a setup for a comeback. As Tony Robbins says, "Don't let disappointment defeat you; let it drive you!" When our heroes in movies get knocked down, what do we do? We cheer them on to get back up! We applaud their fortitude, their endurance, and their resolute determination. We praise their daring ability to rise and carry on. We must use our audacious fearlessness to do this for ourselves.

Realize that in the game of life you can start over as many times as you need. If something isn't working, switch gears and move on. Intrepidness is not senselessness. Don't be held hostage by the things you can't change. If you can't do anything about it, then let it go.

Altering your course can sometimes lead to new discoveries. Give yourself permission to not always have it together. Every successful person has been knocked down many times. Success comes from getting back up and dealing with the situation with determination.

I firmly believe the universe acknowledges grit and will help your resolve. I've found that the biggest growth often happens when you're at the end of your rope. Why? Because you're forced to find new solutions or, more accurately, you're worn down enough to finally allow the solutions to come in. I have found that is the true difference. We can paddle like heck fighting against the current to make something happen, or we can simply trust, do the work, and go with the flow to allow it to happen.

INQUIRY: Has there been a challenge that has stifled you to the point of paralysis?

Entrepreneurs live on a roller coaster. The highs and lows, ups and downs are non-stop. After years in business, I learned to shift my mindset from focusing on what was tough and instead focus on what was right. I shifted my perspective and started creating an atmosphere that makes me happy, one that builds on the feel goods. I worked on my mindset, rather than my circumstances, sometimes calibrating myself at a stoplight on the way to an appointment by making a mental list of things I am thankful for. By concentrating on gratitude, I feel solid even when chaos is swirling around me. Focus on the internal, rather than reacting to the external.

There are many days in which anyone in business can find themselves in fight or flight mode. In these moments, I have a visualization that repositions the situation in my head. Let's say there's a tough contract negotiation or a difficult client pushing someone's buttons. The moment I sense that storm, I imagine myself fishing and reeling in the problem. Some fish are bigger than others, but I resolve to not let myself be dragged out to sea. I take control of the problem and do my best to cast out ahead of it, slowly and steadily reeling it in rather than letting it take control of me. That's a pivotal change in attitude. You're catching it. You're not allowing it to catch you.

When Hurricane Irma hit Florida, Naples took quite a beating. During the cleanup and recovery that followed, we had two closings in six months. Two. Even deals that were about to close, couldn't because of property damage. Banks wouldn't sign off on a mortgage when a palm tree was sticking through the roof. I was, once again, starved for cash and eating cereal. I'm not embarrassed. Every entrepreneur has been there.

I've learned that rough times give rise to creativity. Although not ideal, I asked for and received a high interest, short term loan for $250,000. The payoff was $375,000, but it gave me a few months of breathing room. My mantra became, *I have the ability to do what needs to be done.* **There is more than enough. Everything goes right for me.** The interest hanging over my head lit a fire in my belly to generate new ideas and new business. What happened? We secured unanticipated listings and by reaching out to New York brokers, we received a few amazing referrals that saved the day. I miraculously paid off the loans and, with the unforeseen tax benefits, my risky decision was ultimately good business.

Want some extra reinforcement and indispensable wisdom on this? Listen to the "How I Built This" podcast by Guy Raz. It's been a beacon of hope for me when I've been super down. He shares stories of the many difficulties entrepreneurs face. Hearing in their own words how they

"Obstacles are those frightful things you see when you take your eyes off your goal."

Henry Ford

almost lost everything and how they climbed back out has helped me boldly bounce back in times of trouble.

INQUIRY: What is a struggle you overcame or are facing now?

During the pandemic, there was another market collapse. It was March, the height of our season, the time where the largest percentage of our yearly sales occur, our most profitable time of year. Our season got locked down. Business ground to a sudden halt. No showings, no closings, no money. I'm sure it's how Macy's would feel if Christmas was canceled. It was a struggle with the unknown on multiple levels, and fear was rampant. Many companies were laying off employees, but the last thing I wanted to do was let my team go. What was I going to do? I was going to make sure they were taken care of by focusing on getting through the moment, rather than the future. I controlled my personal spending by eating in, again. I bought whatever cereal was on sale whether it was Cinnamon Life, Frosted Shredded Wheat, or Froot Loops and, with toast for lunch, it was quite economical. Unhealthy? Maybe. Necessary? Absolutely.

Rather than sit around worrying, I got up each morning and headed to Ave Maria, a planned community a short drive from my house. Developed by Tom Monaghan, founder of Domino's Pizza, the picturesque small-town centers around Ave Maria, a large steel church that looks like a giant bishop's hat. There are lakes and wildlife, and it's quite idyllic. Every morning, I would get up, drive out and walk the loop to my special spot — my favorite bench at the far side of the lake. I would sit there and think. I found getting outside was good for my inside. I have never felt so connected to my Source. This was my personal turning point. The minute I turned off my car, I would visualize surrendering all my fears, worries, and doubts. In this quiet, I thrived.

During my Ave Maria sessions, I came up with innovative ways to keep my business at the forefront of people's minds. Little did I know that when we came out of the storm, we'd be the first called when the sun was shining. This was the turning point for my company. We used this opportunity to simply create without the typical day-to-day interruptions.

For example, during the crickets of the pandemic, I offered McQuaid & Company marketing team support to some of our local builders and developers. I recognized that they were all dealing with the same fear of the unknown, sitting on valuable homes or communities that had already broken ground. Every day, I made calls to establish or re-establish a relationship and offer behind-the-scenes support. It was a challenge to get print design work done, so we helped with that and their social media, too. Anything they needed. Although many of them simply used the proposition as a "pick your brain" session, the initial no-strings attached conversations generated property to sell. Fast-forward to now and that effort has led to a ton of business for my team and my company. The intent was pure, the offer to help was simple, but the outcome has been an incredible bonus that continues to grow and evolve to this day. It was the seed of what is now our New Construction and Development Division.

I also had more time during the pandemic to network and was asked to speak at a virtual conference for the National Association of Realtors. It was well received, and they did a wonderful article about us in *Realtor Magazine* with a circulation of more than a million copies. To continue promoting our properties, despite the inability to physically show them, we created "Open House" tour commercials of all our listings and ran them on a local cable network. We doubled down on "caring" for our team, delivering fun packages to their homes, and having weekly Zoom calls. We surprised clients with bouquets of flowers and pizzas to brighten their day, a little unexpected delight. We continued mailing to the communities we serve, but did a dramatic pivot in material, offering fun activities that could be enjoyed at home and delivered prizes to those who participated. When our quarantine period was lifted, McQuaid & Company offered "The Greatest Shows," outdoor movies in the promenade outside our office, each themed according to their classic titles. First and foremost, this became a moment to show how we as a company care about our community. The added benefit was that it attracted lots of new business.

Facing these challenges gave my team (and me!) a reason to find hope. We found light in the darkness and most importantly, it gave me the chance to reignite the light from within.

Yep, life will deliver hard knocks. I've certainly had my share, including my dad's long-term solution to a short-term problem. One thing about each of these is that no matter how bad the situation was at that moment, I got through it. Trials and tribulations are never everlasting. The old saying, "What doesn't kill you makes you stronger" is hard learned, but true. Afterall, the brightest diamonds form under the most extreme pressure. Struggles provide the opportunity to prove your mettle. Want to have things turn out best? Then, make the best out of how things turn out.

Storms are a part of life. I've learned to put up my umbrella and be Gene Kelly dancing in the rain. When it begins to get cloudy, that's when I start to look for possibilities. Ask yourself, where are the voids? If there aren't people coming through the door, what can you do to draw them in? If you want people to talk about you, create something remarkable. If you haven't reached out to prior customers in a while, hunker down and do it. This is what we call rainmaking. Sometimes dancing in the rain is not enough, you must make your own.

The hard times have made me realize that no matter what, I can figure it out by betting on myself, double downing if you will, and trusting the Universe will step up and conspire with me to do so. No matter how sad, how hopeless, how punched I have felt, I'm still here. You are, too. And it's time for us to shine.

"Getting knocked down in life is a given. Getting up and moving forward is a choice."

Zig Ziglar

Your first mission
INVEST IN YOURSELF

MISSION 1

It's time to find your intrepidness, to put your armor on and show yourself and the world how strong you are. You want some pluck? Courage? You want to be bold? For this investment, blast "Unstoppable" by Sia on your stereo. Put it on repeat. This is the song you've been waiting for. She's talking to you. You're a force to be reckoned with. Your personal army is going to guard you against anything or anyone who tries to tear you down.

I keep a photo of my young self on my bathroom mirror and talk to it at times, as a friendly reminder of how far I've come. I tell the little girl how proud I am of her and that she is "safe." Find a childhood photo of yourself. Pick a favorite. Are you missing your two front teeth? Did you cut those bangs yourself? Are you wearing your favorite outfit? Remind yourself when this photo was taken, and what your life was like back then. Now, jump forward to the you of today; the you that stares back in your bathroom mirror. **Think of three no good, terrible things that happened to you between the time the childhood photo was taken and now.**

Write them here:

1. _____

2. _____

3. _____

Look! You're still here! Let these be a reminder on what you've overcome and how. Those were probably some hardships and heartache you didn't think you'd get over, right? Guess what? You did. We aren't what happened to us. We are what we've chosen to become. Keep this list handy when you are faced with another circumstance in which you find yourself questioning whether you can get through it. You'll see that you can. You really can!

YOU'RE UNSTOPPABLE.

INVIGORATION

KEY 2

THE ACT OF GIVING LIFE AND ENERGY TO MAKE SOMETHING STRONGER, MORE EXCITING, OR SUCCESSFUL; ACTIVATION, STIMULATION, EXHILARATION.

IT'S WHAT MAKES A DAY EXCITING!

I saw a post on Facebook recently that said, "We only get 4,000 weeks to live."

Rather startling, isn't it?! 4,000 weeks. That certainly puts a number to it. I got out my calculator. That's assuming I'm going to live to 77. I have already had the harsh reality that life is finite. My dad died when I was ten years old, and I got gut punched again when my mom died at just 53. It may or may not be a cosmic coincidence that as I sit here on my Florida sunporch writing these words, I'm 53.

I hear the very real tick of time.

That's why I decided to write this book, and why I feel the importance of waking up every morning with determination and spending my efforts each day doing things that bring me satisfaction. When I put my head on my pillow each night, I answer to myself. I take every day to the INth Degree, really going all in, because I believe not a single one should be squandered. It's always been that way for me. My mom would not allow for less. Growing up, even during summer vacation, she always roused my sister and me by telling us, "You were given this beautiful day. You don't want to waste it." With that said, we were only allowed to sleep in one day a week.

So, in thinking of those 4,000 weeks, rather than being a Debbie

Downer and telling you that death is coming for all of us, let me instead be Polly Positive and say, we're alive! **Let's LIVE!**

Invigoration is the act of giving vitality to make oneself (or someone else) feel fresher, healthier, more energetic, and darn excited to be alive. It's everything that makes a day (and life) exciting. Being

"Be willing to be a beginner every single morning.

Meister Eckhart

bored is boring. We live in a colorful world. We're alive in it! Let's wake up each morning and set out to add extra vibrance to the day.

Lots of people go through the week looking forward to Friday, living five days in anticipation of two. What's the matter with Monday? Why would I dread Monday and not dread Saturdays? Monday isn't the monster hiding under the bed. Monday is the chance to hit the week with a "can do" attitude. Monday isn't just any other day. It's the day where your impact on your business and your world begins. It's an opportunity to set the tone for how the rest of the week will go, but it's a conscious decision to make it so. If you don't wake up on Monday morning with passion for your week and your work, then you better start thinking about why. The same goes with each of the other six days of the week, too.

I want to be invigorated about my day, every day. When I'm energized, I invigorate others, whether clients, my team, or my dog. So, how do I do that?

Each morning I wake up thankful. Hey, I woke up! I've been given the gift of a new day, whether it's Sunday, Monday or Thursday. With a grateful heart, I welcome it. No matter what's going on or how chaotic life is around me (or within me), there must be something worthy of gratitude. I make it my mission to find it, and I encourage you to do the same. Gratefulness costs nothing, but the payout is big. Each day is full of promise and possibility, you just have to seek it out.

TRY IT!	Today is the day to learn something new, to eat something delicious, to do something nice for someone, to reach out to that friend you haven't talked to in a while.
DO IT!	Today is the day to act on something you've been putting off. I look at even a simple act like finally cleaning out those boxes in the attic as a move to better my world.
ENJOY IT!	Today is the day to smile at everyone I can and spread some goodness around.
TRUST IT!	Today is the day I'm moving one step closer to my next big dream.

Rather than being a passive observer, I believe it's my personal responsibility to inject my days with a dose of excitement. This life is mine, and I'm going to make decisions that enrich it. I'm going to push myself forward. I'm not going to wait for life to happen to me. I'm going to go all in to make it happen for me, and I know you're going to make it happen for you, too!

Let's talk about daily routines. Understandably, each person's life circumstances are different. Some people have children to get up, get ready, and get to school. Some people have elderly parents who need their attention. Others have dogs to walk and goldfish to feed. The point here isn't necessarily about a specific routine, but to purposely find one or two things each morning that makes you feel alive, vibrant.

I love the early hours. I'm a "morning person," generally waking around 4 a.m., without an alarm clock. (Crazy to some, I recognize.) After taking

"Write it on your heart that every day is the best day of the year."

Ralph Waldo Emerson

a moment to breathe in a little gratefulness, I get my long-haired Dachshund, Penny, out of her bed. She races to the door and sits, always excited to see what's outside on this new day. I hook Penny's leash onto her collar, pick her up, and we head out the door with expectation. "Good morning, world," I say, with childlike wonder, as I put her onto the grass of my front lawn. "Thank you, God!" While she's looking for the perfect spot, I say my morning mantra: **"I am open to receiving all the goodness, abundance, and love that the Universe has to offer. Amen."** That's my thing, my ritual.

I have a selection of encouraging affirmations to positively frame the way I think and feel about myself and the world. These simple, short phrases are confidence boosting, soul affirming, upbeat thoughts, and I firmly believe they work. There are a lot of successful people who start their mornings with affirmations. Michelle Obama tweeted out the mantra she practices daily: "Am I good enough? Yes, I am."

For a #MondayMotivation on social media, Jennifer Lopez shared that she believes positive thoughts require effort, sometimes even having to force ourselves to do so. She said her daily declarations are part of that mission and revealed to Oprah the affirmations she uses: "I am whole, I am good on my own, I love myself. I love you, Jennifer. I love the Universe. The Universe loves me. God loves me. I'm youthful and timeless at every age. I am... enough."

My co-author Bruce's daily mantra is "God, continue to bless me, so that I may bless others." (And it seems to be working out nicely for him!)

Penny and I come back in for our morning routine. She gets her chew stick and climbs up onto the back of the sofa to delight in it, and I typically plop down with a blanket to relish some time with no outside distractions. It's just Penny and me. I like my morning to set the foundation for a great day, so I'll spend some time looking at or listening to something optimistic to tune my mindset to "it is possible."

INQUIRY: Who do you spend the most time with?
Who do you follow on social media?
Are they invigorating your life?

A favorite go-to is "The Secret" app, inspired by Rhonda Byrne's worldwide best-selling phenomenon. Each post is incredibly powerful, designed to trounce any negative thought patterns and keep readers on track with good thoughts each day. A recent post:

I am feeling healthy and strong today. My body is a vessel of wellness. Today I will focus on what makes me feel good. I am a healthy and happy person.

The posts and aphorisms I read often sit with me, a little whisper that resonates in my soul like when someone shares a heartfelt thought or tells me something that opens my eyes a bit, enlightens me. I love to discover new things, have my mind expanded. I think often about the things people have taught me. It's sometimes the humblest things that have the longest lasting power. There was an old Italian couple, for example, who many years ago lived down the street from me in Youngstown, Ohio. I became friendly with them and, in Youngstown, everything Italian reigns supreme, from pizza to fresh Italian bread. My neighbors were the epitome of their heritage, from the Capodimonte porcelain chandeliers to the constant stream of homemade goodness.

Why do I still think of them all these years later? One of the memories forever etched in my mind was watching the husband, Joe, in the kitchen in an old white t-shirt make homemade pasta, sauce, and meatballs. My mouth waters just thinking about it. Joe shared with me a secret about why his fresh from the garden tomato salad tasted so incredible, so much more delicious than any I'd ever had. He was the first to instruct me that tomatoes are grown in the hot sun and are never to be refrigerated, and then he taught me the secret to cutting them. He showed me how to remove the core by cutting around the stem in a cone, but then to hold the tomato in the palm of your hand and with a paring knife carve chunks out of it in a scooping motion, like melon balling. The logic behind it was passed down to him from his grandmother who explained the pores of the tomato must be opened to receive and absorb the vinegar and oil for a few hours before consumption. A tomato sliced in a downward motion closes off the pores and doesn't allow for the tomato to soak up all the dressing goodness.

"We are what we repeatedly do, excellence then becomes a habit." Aristotle

That "tomato theory" taught to me by my good old neighbor Joe has lived on long after his death. Not only is it how I've cut my tomatoes since, but I also absorbed the lesson as a metaphor for my life. I think about it often. When I'm closed off, closed minded or just simply stressed, upset, or worked up, I'm in no position to take in goodness. Any kind of goodness. I want to be open to receive and absorb all of life's best dressings.

So, with that concept in mind, each morning, before diving down the rabbit hole of emails and social media, I let my positive apps inspire me with quotes of wisdom and then I open YouTube to look for something quick to watch that's motivational.

YouTube's algorithm recognizes me and gives me a curated list of attitude-stimulating options. I often pick what pops up at the top of the recommended list. That can range from Abraham Hicks or Tony Robbins to Oprah. I take the suggestion as a random sign of something I need to hear, learn, or understand.

It is then, when I'm feeling in a great frame of mind, that I deal with the work correspondence on my plate. After that, I get in a swim or a treadmill run, shower, dress, and I walk out the door each morning energized and raring to go. By the time I get in my car, I'm happily invigorated by my affirmations and the positive vibe I've absorbed in my heart and processed with my brain, and I'm prepared to greet the world with optimism and enthusiasm.

On the ride to work, I listen to more good things — for the longest time it's been Abraham Hicks. We'll talk more on this later, but for now, know I might be hearing something like:

This is a good morning. This is a new day. This is a new beginning. This is me choosing my vibrations most deliberately. This is me being me. This is me, new in this day with all kinds of things that are available to me. This is a really good day. In this good morning,

I'm allowing myself more than ever before to be receptive of everything I've intended. This is a good day.

And that's just at one red light! As I make my way into my office, I visualize my team and send them good thoughts for their days. I pull into the garage behind McQuaid & Company and park. I grab my bag, walk to the backdoor, put my code into the electronic lock, and turn the doorknob... *Bam!* The light comes on and through the door walks, "*Tiffany McQuaid, Superstar!*" Or so I tell myself. Sometimes with a whisper. Sometimes with a roar!

My day is often spent planning, marketing, negotiating, and, most importantly, invigorating my team. I lean on my mantra, actively remaining motivated. *This is a good day! This is a really good day!* I will also (over)share that I have a little device I tuck into my bra to give me my own secret superpower. (And, yes, I know it might sound nutty!) Most days, I have a crystal concealed in my bra that gives me a private umph.

Many cultures use crystals to promote a flow of good energy and believe they have healing properties for the mind, body, and soul. One might dismiss the idea as pseudoscience (or a bit out there), but for me, the power of suggestion — and what it does for my mind — gives me a little personal vigor. Depending on my day's needs, I pick a crystal from my collection. Clear quartz is said to be a master healer for the entire energetic system. Jade is for prosperity. I keep a good-sized tiger's eye in my car and on my desk, which is believed to lessen fear and give stamina and abundance.

One day my crystal secret was revealed. In advance of an important meeting with an agent of mine and his builder client, I tucked a small oval nugget of citrine away. Citrine aligns personal power and is said to promote stamina and prosperity. As the meeting concluded, we walked to the

"Don't you find that work, if you love it, is actually really invigorating?"

Cate Blanchett

27

front of the office. I must have moved oddly because I felt it dislodge, slip out of my bra, slide down the inside of my dress, and drop with a clunk onto the floor. The builder looked down and said, "I think you just laid an egg." We all got a big laugh, but my agent landed the deal! That was egg-cellent!

My point here is what could it hurt to find your own surreptitious lucky token that gives you a charge? We all know that some days simply aren't the party we dreamed of, so a little secret charm might just be the thing that gives you the power to make the best of it. *This is a good day!*

INQUIRY: What's your lucky charm?

Another of my invigorating habits is taking a break in my day to get outside and appreciate a moment of Florida sunshine. It's been proven that spending just a few minutes a day in nature increases vitality levels. *Vitality!* That's life!

I can come alive watching seagulls dance over the water or seeing what my mom used to call the "sneaky birds" mimic her nickname with their slow strut across the sand, or simply sitting on a bench and considering the shapes of the clouds as they roll by.

I spent ten minutes recently just outside our office door watching ants do their dance and got quite inspired. I came back in from my nature visit and posted this on Facebook:

I just spent some time with ants. I know we all have our busy lives and business going on, but I just took a breather in my day and watched a whole other real estate enterprise, just outside our office door, second palm tree to the left. Ants get it done! These amazing little creatures wanted me to tell you it's all worth the effort! Push toward your long-term goals. Take your dreams seriously!

Watching these hard-working ants taught me a thing or three:

1) *Ants aren't selfish. In fact, they are very altruistic, ready to give effort where needed.*

2) *Ants exemplify teamwork at its finest. They work together with the same goal in mind, getting that little muffin crumb to the right place.*

3) *Ants dare to solve problems and overcome obstacles, even braving the lead if needed.*

I see why ants have been around for more than 100 million years. They are success stories. Here's to your success story! You can do it! Don't ever think you c-ANT!

INQUIRY: When was the last time you sat in nature and just spent some time observing?

Whatever it takes, find what gets you feeling jaunty. I know that invigorating others and spreading kindness around has a helpful impact on my mood and productivity, and rubs off on those around me, too. Throughout the day, I'm encouraging positivity, not by telling someone to be positive, but by simply being positive myself. I believe a great leader leads by example, being a role model for hard work and an affirmative, can-do attitude.

I share compliments on accomplishments and give helpful thoughts on ideas. I congratulate my team on their strengths and achievements and encourage them through their struggles. When someone does something great, we celebrate. When someone on my team needs help, I give it. I've been with them through marriage and divorce, the sadness of death and the happiness of birth, as well as getting over some of life's hurdles. When a cherished member of my team was having an issue with alcohol, I had a heart-to-heart with him, offering a month off at a rehabilitation treatment center. He came back with a strong foundation and the tools to begin conquering those demons, which has allowed him to turn up the volume on his life, newly invigorated, and going all in.

> "To live is the rarest thing in the world. Most people just exist."
>
> Oscar Wilde

After a full day of energizing others and solution finding, I can't wait to get home. There's a different kind of excitement waiting there. The moment my hand hits my kitchen doorknob, I'm *Tiffany McQuaid, Penny's Mom.*

At night, Penny and I often wrap up the day sitting on my screened porch, doing some thinking. One of the main reasons I bought my house was for the beautiful Ficus tree behind it. It makes the porch feel like a peaceful tree house. That's exactly how I sold it to myself! Believed to be more than 30 years old, its substantial form and arbor of bushy leaves has been a great source of peace and surrender for me. At the base of the tree, I buried Birdie and Bogie, two Dachshunds that were my best friends for more than 14 years. I wanted them to share my special spot.

My tree has the power to center me, and I have it beautifully lit so I can see its massive trunk and architecture even at night. There's a constant flurry of activity with birds chirping and fluttering among the branches and the elegant twinkle of a few strategically placed windchimes that sing through its leaves. The energy I feel sitting under it on my screened porch comes from the perfect setting that calms my mind after a day's cacophony. My tree's incredible root system reminds me to stay grounded, no matter how far or wide I may branch out in my life and career.

There's an old proverb that a tree with strong roots laughs at the storm, but after Hurricane Ian hit in 2022, my tree wasn't laughing. Although it remained standing, the entire top was sheared off and all the branches were mangled like a dish of spaghetti. Several landscapers gave me a gloomy diagnosis, saying the tree couldn't be saved and needed to come down. I refused to accept that and kept asking around. A friend recommended a tree doctor and, although he made no promises, he was knowledgeable and willing to try. After a team of five people worked a half day carefully carving and cutting each branch, then feeding it 35 gallons of nutrients, we waited.

Fast forward six months. I'm sitting here typing these words and looking out at a tree that is recovering, with so much new growth. My tree is invigorated! I once heard Dolly Parton say, "Storms make trees take deeper roots." My tree means even more to me now. I see it as a daily reminder that no matter how things may seem at the time, there is always hope and opportunity for growth, you just have to put in the effort and never forget your roots.

On that note, I end every invigorated day as I started it, with a positive thought for something I'm grateful for and this reminder to myself: **No matter what happened during the day, tomorrow is a fresh start. I'm always excited to see what happens next.**

"Whoever is happy will make others happy too."

Anne Frank

Insight on INVIGORATION

You want your business to be a success? Then, fall in love with your day, each and every one of them. My goal is to vibrate with life. I want that for you, too. When you're having a good day, you're going to help others have a good day, too. By making someone else feel good in their skin, they want to be around you, whether it's people working with you or those buying from you. Invigorating your team with positivity increases productivity. When you're able to energize customers, they are revved to buy what you're selling.

If you're going to The Inth Degree, you should have a mantra or affirmation that reinforces optimism and helps you focus on the good. Here are some options. **Choose one that resonates with you or create your own:**

- o I am successful and confident.
- o I am powerful, strong, and full of light.
- o I am ready to receive love in abundance.
- o I am making a difference in the world.
- o I am deserving of love and happiness.
- o I am capable of achieving my dreams.
- o I am an unstoppable force of nature.
- o I am filled with gratitude for all the good things in my life.
- o I am not defined by my past. I am driven by my future.
- o I am squeezing every ounce of worth out of this day on Earth.
- o All I need is within me right now.
- o Today is a phenomenal day.
- o Note to self: I am knocking your socks off.
- o _____

I've found that saying my mantra out loud helps me internalize the message and encourages my brain to buy into it. Repeating it throughout the day keeps me moving in a constructive direction. Don't knock it until you try it! Really.

INQUIRY: What time do you typically get up?

Let's talk about that morning situation. Perhaps you're not going to be Leonardo da Vinci, who purportedly never slept for more than two hours a day, but you might decide to get up a teensy-weensy bit earlier. (See how I tried to make that sound cute?) Try waking up for a few days just 30 minutes before anyone else in your house or 30 minutes earlier than you normally do. You might find those 30 minutes are your greatest "me" time.

I've learned to love the dawn. I've read about all sorts of proven health benefits to getting up early, including better sleep, more energy, improved wellbeing, increased mental clarity and mental health, and more time to get the day off to a brilliant start. Early risers are often considered problem solvers and leaders. Countless studies tout that healthy adults who wake up early have a more positive state of mind than night owls. Night owls might argue, but most people get more done in the morning than at night.

Sleep experts say it takes a month or so to get into the habit of waking up early, but once you do, you don't even need an alarm clock. Expert advice is to start gradually, waking up a few minutes earlier each day. I have a friend who has always had trouble getting up in the morning, tending to hit the snooze button repeatedly. She now keeps the clock away from her bed so she must get up to turn it off. If that's your sneaky snoozy routine, do the same.

What will you do with your extra time in the morning? You'll find it peaceful, with fewer distractions. It's extra time to set priorities, decide what your day is going to look like, get out ahead of it rather than feeling you're in a constant race to catch up. You might have time to make yourself a healthy smoothie. Take an extra-long shower. Do a little gardening. Get that exercise in! Have some fun with your dog. Make your bed. (So, after a well-run day, it will welcome you home at night like a nice hotel room.)

What are some other things you can do to better your day, your world, and your life? Here are 10 ideas:

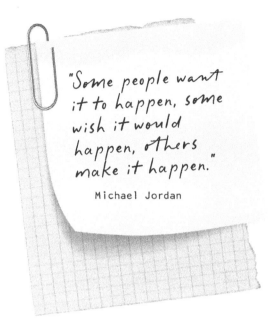

"Some people want it to happen, some wish it would happen, others make it happen."

Michael Jordan

o Eat your lunch outside.

o Spend 10 minutes quieting your mind in meditation. (My two favorite apps to get me going are "Headspace" and "Zen.")

o Find out everything there is to know about one of the flowers in your garden.

o Call your childhood best friend.

o Turn off the TV and turn on your favorite music when you were a teenager.

o Do a deep internet dive into an interesting subject.

o Leave a secret happy note for someone.

o Spend a few hours volunteering.

o Clean out your closet and donate some clothes to a local charity.

o Go pick up litter around your neighborhood.

Now, what else can you do to help organize your day? If you don't plan your time, rest assured that someone else will. To-do lists (and checking items off!) reduce stress and allow for self-congratulations.

Minimize interruptions by turning off your phone and email when you need undistracted creative time. Keep your calendar updated and organized, including reminders for family and friends' birthdays. We have a display monitor in our office that features our team members' special days. I find wishing someone happiness at a life moment brings extra joy to mine. Don't forget to go outside and take that nature break! Come back to your mantra anytime you feel the day is getting out of kilter.

"Give yourself a gift of five minutes of contemplation in awe of everything you see around you. Go outside and turn your attention to the many miracles around you. This five-minute-a-day regimen of appreciation and gratitude will help you to focus your life in awe."

Wayne Dyer

As an ongoing practice, there are other things you can do to keep life rejuvenated. Exercise your creativity by engaging in activities that stimulate you.

Do you like to paint? Get out your brushes and paint!

Like to crochet? Start making your mom a blanket! Being creative unlocks the imagination.

Feeling stuck? Change your surroundings! Sometimes I find just going somewhere that's busy perks me up. You can also do something unexpected. Paint a wall your favorite color. Add something to your office that makes you giggle. I added magnetic eyeballs to the plants in our office and mustaches to some of our outlets! Silly I know, but they spark conversation and bring unexpected smiles. (Look to the Information Guide on Page 161 to see how to get the conversation pieces I'm talking about!)

And never stop learning! Broadening my knowledge helps me think more expansively. Diving down the Internet rabbit hole on a random topic or something that interests me tickles my mind and often helps give birth to new ideas. One of my recent successful ideas stemmed from watching "Taxi TV" during a trip to New York. I typically turn off the sound on the monitor in the cab but left it on to take in some New York noise. In addition to learning about the impending rain, I watched an open house tour for a New York City apartment and realized every real estate market is an opportunity for video home tours. "Open House Near Me" was born. The Naples version is a winner, and we have big plans for the future. Check it out on YouTube! You simply never know when stimulation will hit.

INQUIRY: What is the last thing you did that gave your business a burst of invigoration?

There is one final secret to share on invigoration that anyone can do each day. I can 100% guarantee it will increase your business and life satisfaction. And that is…Smile!

On one of my recent deep internet dives, I explored the power of a smile. I discovered a study from the University of California at Berkeley that compared the smiles of students in an old yearbook to their well-being and their ongoing success. By measuring the smiles in the photos, researchers were able to predict how well each person scored on standardized tests, how happy their marriages were, and how inspiring they were to others. Guess what? The widest smilers consistently ranked highest in every category.

If that's not reason enough, let's give your life more years! A research study from Wayne State University found that the span of a baseball player's smile on his Major League Baseball card in 1952 predicted his life span! Non-smiling players lived an average of 72.9 years, while players with big 'ole smiles lived an average of 79.9 years!

Need more? A study out of Technische University in Munich exposed volunteers to various stimuli then used electromagnetic brain scans and heart-rate monitors to generate "mood-boosting values." One specific stimulus registered as the mood-boosting equivalent of eating 2,000 chocolate bars and receiving $25,000. What was that stimulus? A smile.

A smile is one of the most invigorating and success-inducing actions you can offer yourself and your business. An infectious smile is a magnet. Did you know the smile ☺ is the symbol rated with the highest emotional content in the world? Once our smile muscles contract, there is a positive feedback circuit that sends an electrical signal to the brain that reinforces our delight.

So, smile more. Consider it your life's logo.

And, if you can, wake up a little earlier because, as my mom always said, "You don't want to waste this beautiful day."

"We shall never know all the good that a simple smile can do."

Mother Teresa

Your second mission
INVEST IN YOURSELF

MISSION 2

You want to stand out? Get invigorated! It's time to crank up the volume of your life. I'm feeling good about my day, and I want you to feel good about yours, too. Let's stack the soundtrack with some toe tappers. Here's the run:

"Me Too" *by Meghan Trainor*

"I Feel Good" *by Pitbull*

"Good to Be Alive" *by Andy Grammer*

Put them on your playlist and dance like no one is watching and, if someone is watching, give 'em an incredible show! It's good to be alive! Don't worry... I'll wait here if you want to play one of those over again.

Now, let me tell you about something I do at the beginning of each year. I give the members of my team an old-fashioned diner waitress order pad and tell them to write down what they'd like to order up for the year. We then hang them on our makeshift short order rack for all to see (a clothesline in our Think Tank conference room) and ding a restaurant call bell and say, "Order up!" It's an exercise that helps visualize what everyone wants and announces it to the Universal kitchen. It's proven successful for my team with goals met, records set, and even marriages announced.

For this investment, here's your order pad. **Tell the Universe what you want!**

Order up!

√∖ MCQUAID & CO.

Invest in Yourself

TABLE NO.	NO. PERSONS	CHECK NO.	SERVER NO.
		274007	

TAX

Now, get your appetite ready. Your order is going to be served. Just surrender and trust that it is already yours.

Oh, and what's that mantra of yours again?

INTENTION

KEY 3

AN AIM, A PLAN, A GOAL, A DETERMINATION TO OPERATE A CERTAIN WAY.

IT'S THE PURPOSE!

Put your seatbelt on and come along for a ride in my car.

As I've mentioned, each morning when I drive to the office, I listen to Abraham. So, who is Abraham Hicks?

Abraham isn't a physical human being, but instead can be described as "Source energy" or "vibrational essence," a collective consciousness channeled through Esther Hicks. Abraham is considered both a spiritual and motivational guide for the teachings on the Law of Attraction. Esther and her husband Jerry's work on this topic - conveyed through Abraham - have been featured in many best-selling books, including *Ask and It Is Given*, *The Law of Attraction* and *The Vortex*. I've read them all.

Abraham's teachings are focused on helping people improve their lives by learning how to align their thoughts and emotions with their desires. According to the Law of Attraction, people can attract the things they want in life by focusing on what they want, rather than what they don't want. Abraham's teachings have allowed me to intentionally manifest positivity in my life. I wish I'd realized the power of deliberate intention, good or bad, at the start of my journey. Rather than staying in the spiral of negativity, it's empowering to know I can mentally turn any situation around by focusing on the amazing things I have in my world and business. It's just a matter of bringing forth the good, intentionally. Abundance!

This year I was able to check off a bucket list item by hearing Esther Hicks speak in Miami. It was electric to experience the teaching in person. Abraham asked the gathered crowd, "What's 'trending' in you? Where are you right now?" Abraham explained that just like the viral things we all see trending on the internet, we should know the top things that are trending within us, our dominant thoughts, emotions, and beliefs.

Hmmm, I thought, notebook in hand. **What am I focusing on?**

While driving to Miami, I had been thinking about the impending recession's impact on my company's ability to grow. I was strategizing on the negative aspects. I've faced recessions, hurricanes, and financial strain before, and always landed on my feet, although wobbly at times. I knew I was going to be okay, but I was thinking, *how am I going to get us out of this again and remain standing?*

During the break, I realized I was focusing on the wrong thing. I flipped the recession in my mind. I sat with myself and wrote down all that we as a company had to offer — insight, creative power, dynamic salespeople, money set aside for dark days — and let that trend in my head. *I've already been through this*, I thought. *You have the skills. You can do it. You are solidly planted.* That's when visions of success began trending in me.

I saw a meme on Facebook recently that said, "Easy to spot a yellow car when you are always thinking of a yellow car. Easy to spot opportunity when you are always thinking of opportunity. Easy to spot reasons to be mad when you are always thinking of being mad. You become what you constantly think about. Watch yourself."

"Most people do not realize that thinking about something is inviting the essence of that 'something' into their experience."

Abraham, *The Amazing Power Of Deliberate Intent: Living The Art Of Allowing*

The Law of Attraction says if we are focused on negative thoughts, emotions, and beliefs we will attract more negative experiences into our lives. On the other hand, if our intention is on positive thoughts, emotions, and beliefs, we will attract more positive experiences into our lives. I want to create a more positive and fulfilling life experience, and I'm sure you do, too. The principles and practices I'm sharing with you help set my daily intentions, and it's been transformative for me both personally and for my business.

INQUIRY: What's trending in you right now?

You and I have both lived long enough to know what we want and what we don't want. Let's agree to make it our intention to move in the direction of what we want, toward what we desire. Intention is the starting point of all creation. Our thoughts and emotions are the building blocks of our reality. By focusing on what we want to create and visualizing it as already a part of our lives, we create a vibrational match between ourselves and our desires. The result: we attract the people, resources, and circumstances that bring our intentions to fruition.

Rather than living with a pit in my stomach like I did for so long, I have learned to let go and surrender to the idea that it has always worked out. I worried about things that never came to fruition and my worries never solved anything. What did? Positive action.

With intention there's a catch...

Intention isn't enough on its own. Work is required. We must shore up our desires by being open and receptive to inspired thoughts and ideas, and we must be willing to put forth some effort. Inspired action tells the Universe we are serious about realizing our desires and helps bring our intentions to life.

I heard a story about a Buddhist monk who was invited to speak to a college ethics class. He walked into the room and didn't say a word. He looked at the gathered students all awaiting his instruction, and then went up to the board and wrote: "Everyone wants to save the world, but no one wants to help do the dishes." Everyone laughed. He explained that only a rare few are called upon to do something extraordinary like running into a burning building and saving someone's life. But, he said, it's the smallest acts of intentional kindness — helping an elderly person get their groceries into the car, holding the door for someone, or simply a smile — where we all can make a difference. "Life," he explained, "is our universe," and taking intentional steps to make it better is a profound deed to save the world.

One of my foundational personal intentions is to make others feel special. It's become my everyday habit. I make a conscious effort to recognize others' needs and spot their gifts. By celebrating others, my own life has blossomed and been blessed with abundance. Each of us has a three-pound brain with 100 billion neurons constantly shooting off like fireworks. We can create a beautiful, magical explosion simply by being well-intentioned with our actions, words, and thoughts. The result is a better day for others and for us.

I frequent a local farmer's market. I'm always excited to see a particular bagger at checkout and look for her line before queuing up. Every time she sees me, she says, "Oh, it's you!" And I say, "Hello, best bagger in the history of baggers!" Why do I seek out her line? First, she's infectiously kind and always makes me smile. Second, she goes the extra step for her customers, double tying each bag tight to ensure produce doesn't roll around the car during travel. She isn't doing it because someone told her to. She took initiative to prevent her customers from having a bag of bruised tomatoes. Seeing her and experiencing her good energy is a delight that brings me back time and again. I know I'm going to leave with my delicious vegetables and a smile. There's another bonus. I leave her with a smile, too. It's a tiny moment, but the good intention

"All that counts in life is intention."

Andrea Bocelli

that comes from it travels on with me.

I have been going to a hair salon next to my office for years. I had an epiphany (I refer to them as a Tiffany epiphany) there yesterday about intention. A lady named Maria works in the salon. She's one of several people who shampoo clients' hair. I always hope she's the one who gets me, and yesterday was one of the lucky days. As I waited at the wash station, I noticed two other clients being shampooed. Neither of the other shampooers spoke to their clients. They were just going through the motions, doing a fine job by normal standards, but just getting to the finish line, the end result. It was a noticeably cheerless encounter.

From the moment Maria walked over to me, I felt like the most special person in the room. She delights in her work, humming beautiful melodies while she massages my scalp. Afterwards, she sat me up, wrapped a warm towel around my neck, and gave me a shoulder massage — all while offering sweet words of encouragement. When finished, she said, "Have a beautiful day, my princess." I left feeling like royalty. Maria takes delight in what she's doing, and her intention is clear: make her clients feel good. That is her magic.

Everyone at the salon can share stories about Maria. Her kindness comes from within and radiates out. The point here is when you bestow your work with pluck, people notice. They feel it. No matter your job, if your intention is to complete the task at hand with good-heartedness, whether selling a product or delivering a service, you'll stand out and have raving fans.

INQUIRY: What is something you do to delight your customers?

From my first day as a licensed Realtor® in 2002, my intention was to own my own brokerage. When I started my company, it was already clear to me what voids needed to be filled, and how my firm could differentiate itself from the others. It was my intention to create a new kind of real estate brokerage, one built on doing things differently. My idea was to take the classic real estate model and give it a twist, a punch of color, and a lot of heart.

The actions I've taken to help manifest that intention haven't been easy. While there's something magical about creating something from nothing, you must endure (and overcome) a lot of difficulties to make it happen. I separated from my former business partner while simultaneously enduring a painful separation from my love partner. There was no money, no team, nothing but a dream. Each had to be realized with an unequivocal belief in myself and my vision, while wading through a river of risk, stress, and uncertainty. Each day, my foundation and my saving grace was my intention: wanting to be the best by doing the best.

Writing this 10 years later, I'm on the other side. My goal of being "different" has been realized, but I now understand my real intention is to be of service. We give extraordinary service and make the transaction of buying or selling a home a caring experience. That's originally all I had to give. But it's given us a distinctive edge over the big guys, the national franchises. Our clients notice, come to us again and again, and refer friends and family. Excellent service is about how you treat people, and it doesn't cost a thing.

As our team has grown, we've become a group of people who care about each other. We cheer one another on and have each other's backs. We've created an office that is not "inner competitive," but one that's kind, leads with heart, and has a palpable passion for our clients and ourselves. Individually we're all dynamos. Together, we are dynamic.

Try something. Walk into any business and see how you're received, greeted, and treated. What's the energy like there? If the owner is going all in with intentionally good thought, it will be welcoming, perhaps even exciting. You will

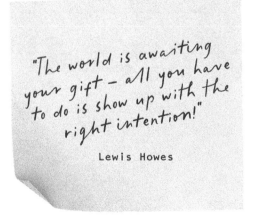

"The world is awaiting your gift – all you have to do is show up with the right intention!"

Lewis Howes

notice a difference between an intentional business and one that is just going through the motions.

In my business, like I do in my home, I intentionally employ all five senses so that my "guests" feel good. I believe that intentionally employing all five senses creates the holy grail of connectivity with a consumer. Engulf them in a vortex of wonderful sensory stimulation that suits your product or service. This simple step is dramatically overlooked in a business environment.

From the moment you step through McQuaid & Company's front door, the experience has been thought through. Even though our primary color is red, there's a Crayola pack of color featured throughout the space. There are inspiring quotes on the wall, like "To be successful, be excellent." And Zig Ziglar's: "People don't care how much you know until they know how much you care." There's neon signage. There's fun framed art. All of it was intentionally chosen to encourage the eye to circulate and land on a point of connection.

We always play a loop of the most popular songs from the past five decades, and at a higher decibel level than most other businesses. Think of when you're somewhere and a song pops up that makes you feel jazzed. What's your first reaction? "Turn it up!" Music transports us. While "elevator music" might work to ease your nerves in a closed box, it doesn't stimulate a cheery mood. Imagine how much more enjoyable it would be, for example, to have your teeth cleaned to tunes from The Temptations or Katy Perry instead of bland background music or the gnawing sound of a drill. My dentist hands me an iPad that lets me select the music. That's thought through. Intentional! And definitely makes the visit more desirable!

Think of the last time you made a call to a company and got the recording, "Press 1 for…," "press 2 for…," "press 3 if you don't think number 1 or 2 will do it." You say, "Operator," in that certain tone. Then repeat it with extra emphasis: "OPERATOR." You wait. What's the hold music? Is it uplifting? Soothing? Too loud? Someone purposely selected that music, or perhaps not. When you do finally get an actual person, how is that first "hello"? The script they read was thought through, too.

Or, again, maybe not. When the call is done, do you feel better or worse about that business? Was it a thoughtful experience?

The use of smell in real estate has been widely discussed. Baking cookies before a showing to kindle a warm, "homey" feeling. There is nothing better than walking through a door and smelling something wonderful cooking. Scent elevates our level of comfort and, therefore, connectivity. Even if the home is not a right fit, if it smells good, it's a memorable visit. Other businesses haven't caught on to the fragrant real estate magic, but think through it in yours. Remember the smell of books in a library? The waft of bread baking in a bakery? The crisp perfume of fresh flowers in a floral shop? You are transported when you visit McQuaid & Company. Our offices are infused with a specially designed scent called "Happy Home." We have made candles in the scent, too. Isn't creating a positive experience what we're all looking for in business? That's intentional.

When it comes to building and growing your business, taste is one of the easiest ways to stand out over your competitors. My nail salon gives out the best mints! I leave happy. I had a favorite pizza place in Naples. Each time I'd go in, they'd bring a handful of Dum-Dum suckers with the check. It was a little novelty that brought a smile and sparked some fun trading at the table. Anyone want to swap a grape for a root beer? It might sound Dum-Dum, but it was an intentionally sweet moment, and the place was always packed. Fast forward to when a new manager was hired. The Dum-Dums are now in a heavy clay pot at the checkout counter, displayed like tightly planted flowers, and the check is just dropped on the table. The place is no longer crowded, and no one is taking the Dum-Dums. I've noticed the same ones are in the same spot above a crack in the pot. Call me a sucker, but the delivery of that simple lollipop elevated the experience. Is it why they are no longer crowded? I'm thinking it's a systemic

"We do not remember days, we remember moments."

Cesare Pavese

48

transformation. The person with good intentions has gone. I'm sure the manager thinks the packed pot of suckers looks pretty, but it's not inviting. The delivery is off. A good intention with a bad approach can yield the opposite of what you want.

In our offices, visitors are greeted by jars of nostalgic candy. This instantly evokes a good memory and helps a prospective client feel comfortable with us and our organization. I can't tell you how many times I've heard, "Oh, my gosh, I haven't seen a Bit-O-Honey since I was twelve!" For our open houses, we have "take-away treats" as part of our collateral material. Our favorite delights are the mini-Bundt cakes made by a local baker. These are individually wrapped and branded with our logo. The baker gets a plug for her delicious business, and we give a take-home treat to prospective buyers. It's a win-win and far more memorable than a business card. There is incredible power in making a mind/belly connection. That's intentional.

INQUIRY: What's a little something extra you give your clients to let them know you're thinking of them or to become memorable?

In today's post-pandemic world, touch is a little different. Some people are overly cautious about shaking hands, so be thoughtful. If you are shaking someone's hand, do so solidly, while looking in their eyes for instant connection. I'm a hugger, likely playing catch up because I came from a family of non-huggers. Sometimes people really need a hug. Hug deprivation is an actual thing. I've researched it. Hugs reduce stress, lower blood pressure, improve sleep, and build trust. Hugs are healing, but I know they aren't for everyone. Ultimately, if done with consideration, touch can be the seal that binds a business relationship for years to come. If it feels awkward, your trademark smile can be just as connecting.

When we visit potential clients, we are in their space. That offers an opportunity for intention, too. For listing appointments or anytime we're going into someone's home, when greeted at the door, my team knows to look down and wipe their feet before stepping in. The minute you look down, the host knows you're a respectful guest, valuing them and their property. When you look up after doing so, you're already elevated in their minds. Message intentionally delivered. Let's call it the "respect quotient." We also always sit at their kitchen table, not in the formality of the

"When our actions are based on good intentions our soul has no regrets."

Anthony Douglas Williams

living room, to make our presentation and talk together. That's intentionally chosen as it is the heart of the home.

For my listing appointments, I made a deal with one of my favorite florists in town. They make these adorable arrangements of carnations that look like a soda cup with a straw and cherry on top. Shortly after I leave an appointment, the florist shows up with these flowers and a little card that says, "Thank you for sharing your beautiful home with me. Working with you will be a real treat." That intentionally gives them a reminder of me for days to come. By the way, I don't mind that I'm revealing my playbook to my competitors. **In my view, the more good intentions in the world, the better.**

Let's talk about how to intentionally respond to and treat others.

My business didn't become a success based on our beliefs. We're successful because of our actions, our intentional behavior, about those beliefs. We each have power over our experience. McQuaid & Company's approach to our work is from a place of compassion, kindness, understanding, and a desire to always do the right thing. No matter how wonderful we think we are, how we treat people is our secret sauce.

Let me tell you a story about how our firm operates with good intention. We had a closing that went awry. Murphy's law that "everything that can go wrong, will go wrong" ruled the day. A home-buying couple was spitting-nails mad. They felt the builder on this new construction home failed to deliver on promises and we, unfortunately, were caught in the crossfire.

The closing should have been a happy moment for all involved.

Instead, it became a most horrible scene, culminating with the wife in the relationship standing up in our conference room and casting spells on Nicholas, our Vice President of Operations. She literally voodooed him, gesturing wildly with her hands and wishing him to have five heart attacks in one year. For real. During the hubbub, I was at the dentist and missed the scene, but it was so bad, and Nicholas was so shaken we had the office infused with bad energy clearing sage the following morning.

I also reached out to the husband. But before doing so, I thought through my intentions. What did I want for us, and what did I want for him? What was I aiming for? Satisfaction for all parties. I wanted the couple to be happy with their home and wanted McQuaid & Company happy that we helped them manifest their desire for a beautiful house in Florida. "Hi," I said. "It's Tiff..."

The verbal onslaught began. The husband was fired up, and his tongue was rattling. I gave him a few moments to burn while I played Abraham's *This is a good morning!* mantra on repeat inside my head. When he finally came up for air, I said, "I hear what you're saying. I want you to be happy and to love your house. We will get your punch list done, but please help me understand what transpired yesterday that would cause ill wishes on Nicholas's life. He's an employee of mine, and he had nothing whatsoever to do with building the house."

There was silence. Then, he said, "I'm not able to talk about this right now. Let me think about it, and I'll get back to you."

The bomb was defused. When we spoke again, though there was no apology, he calmly delivered his punch list. I'm thrilled to report that he and his wife are happily living in their home, and the year ended without Nicholas having a heart attack.

"Be the reason someone feels
welcomed, seen, heard,
valued, loved, and supported."
Anonymous

Acting with good intention saved the day. Both in life and in business not everything goes perfectly, leaving us struggling sometimes to find happiness in a moment, but if our intention is to look for the positive, we discover it.

Now, let's address the intentional elephant in the room. Sometimes, when people don't know you or your track record, they may not trust your intentions as pure. They may question if you are truly genuine or see your actions as manipulation. The cold, hard fact is that we've all been duped a time or two. When we experience disappointment, we can become jaded and think that someone might be out to "get us," to one up us, or to look out solely for themselves and their needs. We're going to stay true to our good hearts and intentions, despite those judgments and misjudgments.

It's been 20 years since my mom Belinda passed away from ovarian cancer. She always told my sister and me that "no characteristic could be more important in life than a giving heart." After her diagnosis, unbeknownst to us, she started filling a journal for each of her two daughters, recounting memories as they came to her and giving us little reminders of the good-hearted people she'd mothered us to be. Through her writings, it is clear her intention was to be around for much more of our lives and to get to watch our journeys unfold, but ultimately, that wasn't to be.

Thankfully, her journal lives on, and her handwritten recount of some of my life's notable moments and special musings have become a source of joy and great comfort for me. So, her intention to live on... has. When I need a little dose of "Mom," I pull it out and read some of her entries or simply admire her beautiful handwriting.

The cover of the journal is adorned with watercolor dragonflies, which are a symbol of change, transformation, and self-realization. In many cultures, a visiting dragonfly is said to be a guardian angel. The cover reads: "IMAGINE — **In every moment there are a thousand miracles.**" I'm sure she relished finding the perfect book and knowing she was leaving her good thoughts in it for me.

Since my intention here is to help you manifest a wonderful life, let me share lessons my mom's journal gave to me:

1. Give from your heart.

2. Always seek to do great things.

3. Make loads of memories.

4. Never be angry at God's plan.

5. Always be learning.

6. Enjoy moments with those you love.

7. Find things and people that make you feel comforted.

8. Treasure happiness.

9. Love is endless and timeless.

She considered these life lessons and used the journal to share her thoughts on them, often accompanied by her introspection and advice. One of the reflections she shared with me is: "I think your desire to please and do good for others is so strong that it can come back to hurt you when you feel unappreciated or taken advantage of. Try to fight those urges to feel hurt. Take strength in knowing your heart and intentions are always in the right place."

It's true. At times I've felt people haven't trusted my good intentions initially, questioning my sincerity. I've followed my mom's guidance and taken strength in knowing my own heart. Building my business on that foundation, despite the doubters, has proven successful. Why? The proof is in the pudding. People begin to see the results of someone's consistent good intentions, and a reputation is born. An excellent reputation — one that yields trust, loyalty, and happy clients who like to brag — delivers robust business and a happy life.

We're all making constant choices. Life is full of them. Our responses and actions should lead to positive resolution rather than negative escalation. It's giving the voodoo couple another chance, instead of fueling their fire. It's being kind when a loyal employee has a bad day or reacts in a less than desirable manner. It's finding power and strength in silence, stepping away from an argument as opposed to leaning in.

You might have heard the story of the old Cherokee who is having a conversation with his grandson about life. "A fight is waging inside me," he told the boy. "It is a horrible fight between two wolves. One wolf is evil. He is full of bad things like anger, envy, greed, arrogance, guilt, resentment, inferiority, superiority, lies, and ego."

His grandson looked at him wide-eyed. "What about the other wolf?" he asked.

"The other wolf is good," the old Cherokee continued. "He is filled with joy, peace, love, understanding, kindness, generosity, compassion, humility, truth, and faith. The same fight is waging inside every person and inside of you, too."

His grandson thought about it for a moment and then asked his grandfather the question we all want to know: "Which wolf will win?"

"The one you feed," his grandfather replied.

Feed the good wolf. We do that by not just having good intentions, but by acting on them.

INQUIRY: When was the last time you wrote heartfelt thoughts to someone special in your world?

Every year on my birthday, I evaluate and reevaluate my purpose. As I write this, today happens to be my birthday. I'm sitting on the porch of a little villa I rented in Key Largo looking out at the ebb and flow of the ocean waves and pondering the ebb and flow of my own life experience.

I've decided that this is "THE" year. This is the year that all my hard work, ambivalence, indifference, fear, uncertainty, doubt, pain, feelings of "stuckness," stress, and not wanting to make waves will morph into adaptability, trust, surrender, appreciation and going all in on my own power and belief in me. I'm going to double down on my true Self. It's a lightbulb moment that has (probably) come with age. I cannot be the person I used to be and the person I desire to be at the same time. I have the humility and the option to change course rather than sticking to a path that may have been a wrong turn.

"When you were born, you cried and the world rejoiced. Live your life so that when you die, the world cries and you rejoice."

Cherokee proverb

It's a weird moment. I am now at an age where I've lived longer than both of my parents were on this earth. So, my intention this year, at this life intersection, is to celebrate what I have already created. I will no longer continue "surviving" in a day-to-day way. I will direct that timeworn "traffic" elsewhere and will develop the courage to throttle my engine to live my best life authentically and proudly. This is the best gift I could give myself. There is no time like the present. I already feel the wind in my hair!

MAKE YOUR INTENTION TO FEEL THE WIND IN YOURS, TOO.

Insight on INTENTION

So, how do we recognize and set a good intention? A good intention is a desire to do the right thing based on kindness, compassion, and a hope to make things better. Intention isn't a goal-based achievement. Intention is bigger than a goal. A goal comes from the mind. Your intent comes from the soul. A goal is a box to check off. An intention is a powerful purpose to realize.

What do you bring to the dinner table? To the office? To a friendship? To your relationship? Are you focused on problems? The negative? Then, that's what you're bringing to the room.

Is your intention for things to go well? For great things to happen? Then, that's the vibration you're passing along to everyone you encounter.

Remember the Buddhist monk I told you about who suggested to a classroom full of students that everyone wants to change the world, but no one wants to help do the dishes? It's unlikely that our day is going to present us with a burning building and people to save. It's really the little things we do that can better the world and our own existence. What we do, how we act, the energy we share affects everything and everyone around us in tiny, but grand, ways. The butterfly effect... small vibrations can change the world and us. We grow by making little differences. Every decision we make shifts the Universe.

You don't become a better person because of your beliefs. You become a better person because of your behavior. Actions speak louder than words or, as Ben Franklin put it, "Well done is better than well said."

All of us can benefit from a little dusting of kindness. Life is hard. We should all wear a "Handle with Care" sticker. So, check yourself before making a negative comment to someone. Ask yourself, "What will I gain?" There is plenty of unhappiness in the world, do you need to add to it? No matter how wonderful you intend to be, how you treat people tells all.

I've found that **the happiest people aren't the ones who are getting more, but really those who are giving more.** One of my most fulfilling intentions is to find ways to "surprise and delight" others.

A favorite organization in Naples is a youth non-profit that provides home, hope, and healing to abused and neglected children and teens in Southwest Florida. While on a tour of their facilities, I met their delightful Chef Lou, an adorable man with a heart that sits clearly on his sleeve. He spends his day cooking for the kids and told me that his ultimate goal is to have his own pizza oven and do a pizza party for the kids. In speaking the idea, his vision of delighting them was palpable. I got back to the office and ordered two countertop commercial pizza ovens, all the fixings for a magical pizza party, and a "Best Pizza Maker" shirt for Chef Lou. When I delivered the gifts, Chef Lou teared up, and I felt such joy knowing the fun he and the kids would have. Sometimes stopping to listen is the best intention. Listen to how you can help. Small acts of kindness are not just good for others. They are shots of adrenaline in your own heart.

We've all heard about Starbucks' "Pay It Forward" moments where drive-thru customers pay for the drinks of the person behind them in the queue as an act of goodwill, hoping that the goodwill chain continues person after person. These random acts of kindness, done with no thought of receiving anything physical in return, are powerful. Why? They evoke an unexpected smile from the recipient. They also deliver a higher level of happiness in ourselves, a "helper's high." It's a proven fact. A Stanford University study found that students who carried out five random acts of kindness each week reported greater life happiness than the control group. Quite simply (or quite magnificently), we feel good when we do good.

So, what are we waiting for? We have the power within us to set a positive wave in motion and make the world a better place. So, let's make a pact. The next time we see a driver trying to merge into our crowded lane at rush hour, we'll make room. The next time we see someone struggling with packages at the supermarket, we'll help them. The next time we see an expired parking meter and a traffic officer coming, we'll throw in a few coins. The next time we get our cappuccino on the way to work, we'll leave a generous tip for the barista. The next time we're eating a fancy lunch out, we'll call a local school that afternoon and pay off a child's overdue lunch account. The next time you're making dinner, make a little extra to share and delight an elderly neighbor or friend.

"When we feel unhappy, when we feel inadequate, we get stingy; we hold on tight. Generosity is an activity that loosens us up. By offering whatever we can — a dollar, a flower, a word of encouragement — we are training in letting go."

Pema Chödrön,
The Places That Scare You

Making a difference in someone else's life will, in turn, make a difference in ours. A University of Michigan study of 400 elderly couples over a five-year period found that kinder people live an average of five years longer than others. Acting on good intentions strengthens your immune system and expands your life. Quite simply (or again magnificently), making someone's day makes your own.

Rather than being intentional, much of the world works in the realm of distraction and reaction, dwelling in the negative. What we don't have. How we failed. What someone else has done or not done. When we operate on our good intentions, we avoid looking outward to find something or someone to blame. We're able to concentrate on making sense of what's inside of us.

The one thing I can do something about is my own vibration. That's my power. I can feed the good wolf and take sole responsibility for my experience, even when faced with situations beyond my control. Intention is a conscious decision that gives strength, personal reliability, and purpose. **I intend to use my energy and resources to serve the greater good. Want to join me?**

INVEST IN YOURSELF

MISSION 3

It's time to crank up that stereo. Next on The INth Degree playlist is "Rise Up" by Andra Day. Play it loud and proud. It's time to rise up. Rise like the day. Rise unafraid! Amidst life's chaos, we need to find compassion and kindness for ourselves. In doing so, we will be able to share our wonderfulness with others.

Zig Ziglar, one of my favorite motivational speakers, said, "One small positive thought can change your whole day." **So, list 5 things you like about yourself.**

1. _____

2. _____

3. _____

4. _____

5. _____

Now, write your intention for your day or for the coming months:

See those positive thoughts that you like about yourself above? Those are what's going to help manifest your intention.

YOU'VE GOT THIS.

INSPIRATION

KEY 4

THE MENTAL STIMULATION TO DO, TO FEEL, TO CREATE, AND TO TAKE ACTION: ENCOURAGEMENT, EXAMPLE, INSIGHT, MOTIVATION, STIMULATION.

IT'S THE REASON WHY!

Inspiration is contagious. Thankfully, I've caught it at several decisive points in my life.

Shortly after getting my real estate license and joining a Naples real estate office in 2003, the magic algorithms of Amazon recommended that I buy a book: *Use What You've Got & Other Business Lessons I Learned from My Mom* by a woman named Barbara Corcoran. I had no clue who she was. This is well before *Shark Tank*. Back then, her claim to fame was that she created, owned, and had just sold for mega-millions the largest residential real estate firm in Manhattan. She seemed legit and, with my mom's recent passing, the title resonated with me.

I read that book in one night, absorbing its wisdom like a sponge. Barbara's marketing brain spoke to me. She turned a $1,000 loan from a cheating boyfriend into a billion-dollar business. Each of her stories gave me the courage and inspiration to be my most daring self:

"Use your imagination to fill in the blanks."

"You have a right to be there."

"Jumping out the window will either make you an ass or a hero."

Barbara's book was the jolt I needed to begin my journey to open my own business.

After reading the book, I emailed Barbara. I'd never reached out to someone who was "known" before. I explained that I was just starting in the real estate business, that her book was incredibly inspiring, and I appreciated her "outside of the proverbial box" marketing brain. I told her I'd love the opportunity to talk to her. It was a bit bold, a little daring, but what was the worst that could happen? Barbara could have ignored me or simply said no. Those who succeed, especially in sales, knock on the 11th door after the first 10 have closed. Sure, "no" is not the easiest word to hear, but the sting only lasts for a minute. So, why not ask?

One of the best predictors of success in life is the willingness to ask for what you want. Sometimes instead of the dreaded "no," you hear the magic "yes!"

When Barbara's name appeared in my inbox, my eyes wiggled in their sockets. At first, I thought it was an automated reply. It wasn't. Barbara responded specifically to some of my ideas and asked me about the real estate market in Florida. She also opened the door to further conversation, encouraging me to share some of the things I was doing to promote myself in my new real estate adventure. Busy people often are the ones who will find the time to offer wisdom and help.

Her encouragement was invaluable, life-changing really. Starting my real estate career was one of the most vulnerable times of my life. I was a "fish out of water." New to Florida. New to real estate. Up until I made the transition, I was working as a vice president of a marketing, promotion, and special event management company I had co-founded. I was doing back-to-back events and the pressure of the ups and downs of producing one after another was wreaking havoc on my quality of life.

When my fiancé Lou and I decided to relocate to Florida, I took the opportunity to make a momentous shift. Marketing was in my blood. It was what I knew, but real estate had always been a passion. For years, I had been going to open houses for fun and, when we moved to Florida, I successfully sold our investment properties in Ohio "by owner." I found I enjoyed lining up the dominoes to make that happen.

What I discovered, however, after I got my license and entered my first year of real estate, was a lot of self-doubt. *Why did I do this? What was I thinking? Can I really make a career of this?* I was starting from scratch. No experience. No knowledge of the area. No Rolodex filled with heavy-hitting names. My head and heart jockeyed for top position that first year. My head said, *"You're crazy."* My heart said, *"You can do this!"*

I was fortunate during that acclimation to have been taken under the wing of a wonderful broker, Ann, who was incredibly supportive. It was a tough time. I had just lost my mom to ovarian cancer, and Ann became a wonderful friend and mentor, always present and available. Realizing that knowledge is power, I asked a lot of questions and read every real estate related book I could find. Before I had listings of my own, I would sit open houses for agents in our firm and, while waiting on clients to come, I would read industry related material. When people arrived, my mind was already actively in the game, not perusing a *People* magazine. It's a habit I have continued. For my daily exercise, I'd power walk around my "Quail Creek" community, examining each house, memorizing the address, the layout, the front elevation, so that I became the expert when and if the homeowner was ever in the market to sell.

Somehow, I managed to earn $26,000 my first year, and by the end of my second, I had made more than $100,000. That's a testament to hard work, but also being in the right environment to empower my success. Ann continued to give inspiration, helping me build a solid foundation and encouraging me to believe in what was possible, despite my novice capabilities. My adoration for her grew, and she showed me how, despite the competitive industry we were in, to cheer others on. At the five-year mark I had proven my mettle and we joined forces, repositioning the firm as a partnership for another five years.

During this time, as my career started to blossom, Barbara Corcoran was becoming the national real estate expert. When she began contributing to the *Today* show, we corresponded a lot. She would pick my brain about the real estate market for her TV segments and coach and cheer on my marketing ideas and strategies.

I shared with Barbara that I was having a tough time figuring out the next steps of how my life and career should evolve. I was building my client base and using myself as a guinea pig for new marketing concepts, with the goal of using them one day in my own agent training program, but I didn't know how that could happen. I had come to realize that the current situation — wasn't my ultimate aspiration, and I was not living up to what I knew was my potential. I needed something more. Even though I would often have 20 listings on the market, I felt stuck, stuck like a barnacle on a whale, gliding along, but without my own direction.

 INQUIRY: What's your big dream?
Do you believe it to be possible?

In the spring of 2012, a friend told me about a movie called "Katy Perry: A Part of Me." She had seen it with her teenage daughter and said I needed to see it. She thought it would be inspiring to me because Katy's over-the-top approach to life reminded her of mine. Part-biopic, part-concert film, the documentary chronicles Katy's life and rise to stardom and, though I had heard her name, I had no idea of Katy's music or her story. I grabbed a friend who also didn't know much about Katy, and on a Saturday afternoon, we settled into seats near the front of an empty theater, buckets of popcorn in our laps.

From the movie's opening moments, I was captivated. Katy's childhood, career and personal life are dazzling displays of intense imagination, a quest for fun, and true vision. It felt like Katy was speaking, well, singing to me. I'd never seen someone as bright and colorful. Call me an adultescent, but in her songs, her humor, her living, I could relate. She was expressing what I'd felt all my life — striving, dreaming, working, creating, and even sharing the pain of a recent break up due to infidelity. In Katy, I found inspiration! Undeniably, I have a colorful imagination that some might say leans to the schticky, so Katy's world resonated with me. She was able to stay true to herself and turn the vision in her head into something great.

Barely 20 minutes into the movie, I was hooked. Katy Perry proved to me that she was standing out by going all in on her dream.

Be true to you and you can be anything!

Near the end of the movie, Katy's performance of "Firework" got me super emotional and still gets me every time I watch it. Often, to give my morning an extra dose of "Yeah!," I still pull up that movie clip when I'm running on the treadmill. I'm known at my gym for it. (This incidentally caught the attention of a trainer who is now one of my superstar agents.) It's not just the song, it's the movie moment. Katy is singing her heart out, and they cut to her mom in the audience, who looks very similar to my mom. She's clapping and cheering her daughter on. That scene is motivational meditation for me and always leaves me feeling like my sweet mother is still cheering me on.

"Firework" is an infectious song directed towards people with unrealized potential, an anthem for never giving up, even when things are tough. The song opens with a question: "Do you ever feel like a plastic bag drifting through the wind, wanting to start again?" The plastic bag is symbolic of people who waft through life spiritless, without direction. The bag drifts on the wind, having lost its sense of purpose, floating along wherever the breeze takes it. The lyrics encourage that we all have this fuel inside us to make our mark. We just need to light the fuse and find our amazing reason to be.

Katy, a sheltered daughter of born-again ministers, made her originality her blockbusting feature. The entrepreneur in me recognized her gift in defining and celebrating her unique selling proposition. Her originality and smart thinking are an inspiration for exploring new paths to create opportunity (and generate income!)

This little barnacle left the movie inspired to act on my dreams, to let my colors burst, to have my life sparkle and show 'em what I'm worth. In December 2012, I flew to New York to meet Barbara, who had by that time become a well-loved, advice-giving Shark. I

"Be yourself; everyone else is already taken."

Oscar Wilde

walked into her office with what I called my "Barbara Bible," a collection of her wisdom and the marketing concepts she had inspired. It was in that meeting, shortly after "hello" that she announced, "I want to help you, but the value in the business is you. It's time to sever the partnership."

My jaw dropped. I told her it seemed risky and that I was scared to make such a bold move. "Don't wait until you feel courageous," she said. "You'll find the courage mid-air once you jump off the cliff. What's the worst thing that could happen? You could fall flat on your ass, but at least you will have tried." We talked through how that would look. It was December so the market in Florida was heading into its busy season. She encouraged me to tell my partner now, but to set a future date after the season to make the move, so as not to leave her in a lurch.

INQUIRY: Who encourages and inspires you because you see aspects of them in yourself?

I went back to Florida and had the very difficult conversation with Ann. As Barbara had coached, I explained that we were at different stages of our careers and journeys, and I felt the need to start my own venture, to light the fuse of my own firework. We agreed to a May 2013 date and, to prevent rocking the boat, we decided we'd share the news with our agents after the busy season. It made for a kinder, gentler transition.

In May 2013, "McQuaid & Company" was born. I leased office space, hung my red and black sign, started bringing on agents, and put my marketing concepts in place. One foundational business principle for me has always been "giving back" to the community. So, I immediately set out to both do something good and attract attention to my new business. I began thinking of different ways to raise awareness in a crowded market. Although I can't carry a tune, I created a concert series for our town called "Rockin' on the Bay." In my prior career of marketing and event management, I had done a similar series in a town up north, and thought it would be a great fit for our beautiful setting and what I was trying to accomplish here. It became the little concert that could, growing to epic proportions, with more than 5,000 people gathering in the streets in front of our offices for each performance.

My intention was to create something that would build top-of-mind recognition for our area and its businesses. In my naivety, there was an unanticipated obstacle to overcome. A few residents who lived in the mixed-use, waterfront area of town began bad-mouthing my company and me personally. They showed up at City Council meetings with the mean-spirited goal of shutting down the concerts, and more, destroying my company. There was a lot of venom, and it attracted a heap of local media attention. People began referring to it as the "Footloose" situation, a nod to the 1984 movie where a kid (played by Kevin Bacon) attempts to overturn a preacher's ban on dancing in his small town. I was distraught over the bad press and reached out to Barbara for advice. She told me, "Unless you murder someone, steal or do drugs, no media is bad media for your business." But still, my heart hurt.

Even though I knew we were doing the right thing — offering a fun experience in our special setting on the Bay — dealing with these Negative Nellies was a bit overwhelming and confusing.

"*Tiffany*," Barbara wrote me in an email, **"Ignore the naysayers on everything. Anything fresh and innovative makes them uncomfortable and their unintentional job is to clip your wings!"**

Those words have gotten me through some tough times, and I hope by sharing them they will do that for you, too. One thing is certain: everyone has an opinion and when you do something different or exciting, you can expect a lot of feedback, both good and bad. I was frantic that it was going to sully the real estate company and reputation I'd been working night and day to build.

During all of this, I was keeping staff needs met and carrying a heavy financial load for my new upstart. There simply wasn't enough revenue coming in, so I got back out there, took listings, showed buyers around, and did whatever it took to keep the lights on. My head and heart were torn by the stress, and I was physically exhausted.

It was a scramble to keep us going, and a feat to walk through the office door each morning wearing a smile, as though I didn't have a care in the world. Truth be told, I was in a tailspin of despair. I felt like there was no-way-out. My energy was dwindling, and I didn't know which obstacle to tackle first.

Although I could clearly see the vision of what I was trying to do, it started to feel like the puzzle pieces didn't fit and perhaps I'd made the wrong decision. Self-doubt had wrapped her gangly limbs around my neck. If you've ever met her, you know she's a formidable opponent and often when she grabs hold, shows no mercy. Like many entrepreneurs in the formative stages, I began questioning everything. Was this what I was meant to do? Was I doing it "right?" How was I going to pay my bills? The worry left me struggling to accomplish the smallest task and then, once I did, it was a battle to muster the energy to jump over the next hurdle. I felt swallowed. Quite simply, I was losing my hope. And that's very un-me.

One morning amid all the noise, my eyes opened at 4 a.m. and something told me to get up and go. In desperation for answers, I decided to set out looking for guidance, in quest of some revelation for better days ahead. I got in my car and proceeded to the beach with the goal of quieting the noise in my head and releasing my fears and doubts to something bigger than me. *Who knows? Maybe I'll find a message in a bottle,* I remember thinking as I pulled into the public beach parking lot. I climbed out of the car and walked toward the water.

To this girl from Ohio, the ocean is exhilarating and never loses its magic, a beguiling force with a limitless flow of freedom, both majestic and ominous. I plopped my butt down on the sand and looked out at the endless pool in front of me, glowing in the moonlight, and I just listened. The hypnotic murmur of the waves crawling to shore calmed me. It was dreamy.

In that moment, the moment my anxious brain finally took a rest, I asked for guidance. I asked for a sign. *Please give me something to let me know that I am on the right path, that I should stay the course.*

I specifically asked for a sign that I would know or recognize. Then, I surrendered and trusted. It was the very first time I had ever asked the Universe for such a sign.

"What lies behind you and what lies in front of you, pales in comparison to what lies inside of you."

Ralph Waldo Emerson

I left the beach. The sun was rising, and the parking lot was empty, except for my car. I brushed the sand off myself and climbed back into the driver's seat. I headed down the road and crossed our main intersection at Highway 41. As I drove through the juncture, out of the corner of my eye, I saw a white plastic bag, gracefully drifting out of nowhere. It was floating around the air like an untethered, wandering kite. The bag came toward my car, delicately caressing my hood, where I could read its red lettering through my windshield: "thank you thank you thank you thank you." It disappeared for a moment and then reappeared in my rearview mirror, floating up behind my car into the air behind me. Tears immediately began streaming down my face. That was it, my sign!

The first line in my Katy song! *Do you ever feel like a plastic bag, Drifting through the wind, wanting to start again?* Here it was not only drifting through the wind, but it was hitting my car emblazoned with "Thank You."

It couldn't have been clearer if it had been a billboard on the side of the road: **TIFFANY MCQUAID: IT'S TIME TO SHINE!** Nothing like that had ever happened to me before. All I could say as the white plastic bag disappeared into the distance was repeat its red-imprinted message: *thank you, thank you, thank you.* I wiped the tears from my face. My fuse was relit, and I headed into the office that morning full throttle, ready to ignite the light and be the best version of me. I had my sign.

It was exactly the inspiration I needed to give me a renewed sense of purpose. I wasn't defeated. I was just getting started. I had made a commitment to a group of people and to myself, and I wasn't about to let them down. I was 100% going to be that firework and surround myself with firework people, ones who give life their all.

That was the day I started building my business with extra boom, boom, boom. Neighborhood naysayers could join the party or not. We were not going to stop having one. We became the leader in bringing the community together with attention-getting, first-class events from concerts to parades to the Stone Crab Festival. These occasions put McQuaid & Company front and center in Naples. The Negative Nellies faded away and our town rallied.

Our events have since become a really big thing. We get sponsors to help underwrite the costs, and my team and I put in lots of sweat equity to bring them to life, all branded with our red McQuaid & Company touches. I could have never afforded to build and get my company noticed among the big boys in a traditional route. The events turned the spotlight on us, and we stood out among the longtime heavy hitters. This created an opportunity to take advantage of the media components, wide exposure, and a captive audience. Plus, it's given our community a great time and brought us business. All I needed was that sign for validation and inspiration!

Looking back on that time now feels rather weird. My "all IN" headspace is so different. Today, I could handle all that with much more ease. The naysayers wouldn't even ruffle my red feathers. The white plastic bag moment gave me the motivation to allow my inventiveness and creativity to blossom. My company has grown and is now *known* for its fun.

 **INQUIRY:**   If you were to put sweat equity into something unusual to market your business, what could it be?

Last year, a friend got me an extremely special birthday present that actually inspired this book. Knowing I'd become a huge Katy Perry fan, he announced he was taking me to Vegas to see her residency show: PLAY… and had arranged for me to meet her before the show! When he told me the news, I squealed like one of those girls in

> "You know you're living right when you wake up, brush your hair — and confetti falls out!"
>
> Katy Perry

the audience looking up at sweaty Elvis.

There's nothing quite like Vegas and there's nothing quiet about Vegas. Famous for its casinos, nightclubs, over-the-top hotels, and neon — lots of neon, the Vegas Strip may very well be the sparkliest place on earth. Like New York City, Vegas offers the opportunity to suspend disbelief and dream. It's built on hopes, wishes, desires, and a deferral of reality, a literal oasis in the middle of the desert. Some go to Vegas with the fantasy that they'll bet on the right number, pull the perfect arm, or put all their chips on black at the end of the night and walk away richer than rich. That's not me. Yes, I've heard that going to Vegas and not gambling is like going to a restaurant and not eating, but I wasn't there to gamble. I was there to meet Katy Perry!

So, there I am, standing backstage staring at Katy Perry, waiting my turn to have my moment, what I thought would be a quick chance to say thank you for the inspiration she gave me. She was wearing a hot pink and white leather mini-dress and knee-high white boots. Her energy was magnetic, her aura glowing. When it was my turn, I walked over and before I could say anything, she grabbed my hand and said, "Wow! Your nails! Are they real?!" I have attention-getting nails. They are usually painted white and are solid and substantial.

I said, "Yeah, they're real." And then, as she examined them closely, perhaps questioning my honesty, I launched into my story of how they are a result of me electrocuting myself when I was five years old.

I was building a swing for my Barbie. I had fashioned a seat from a cereal box top and tied two strings to each end. I was walking around the house looking for a place to hang it so Barbie could swing like the sassy gal she is. I went over to my mom's junk drawer. Now, this is the 1970s and every house had a junk drawer and jumbo paper clips were a thing. I took one out of the drawer and decided if I stuck it into the wall outlet, which was the perfect height, my Barbie could do her swinging thing. The moment my little fingers stuck that metal paper clip into that socket was ELECTRIC. It blew me across the room and singed the tips of all my fingers that had been holding the perfect conduit. My mom always said that was why my nails grow long and strong.

"Wow!" Katy said. "When you see how the show opens tonight, you are not going to believe it! You're going to freak out." I suddenly realized I was standing there in my lace-up espadrilles talking to Katy "Firework" Perry in her knee-high leather boots and sharing my electrocution story! Little did I know she was about to give me some of the most powerful inspiration that I've ever received for myself, my life, and my business.

Time was standing still. After telling her about the day at the beach and the white plastic bag, and how it was just the sign I needed to keep going, she grabbed me in a tight hug. "I'm never going to forget that story as long as I live," she said. "You've got something. There's something about you…." Then, she cocked her head back and her eyes widened. "I feel like I'm supposed to tell you something," she said, reaching out for my hands and pulling me close. "It might be weird, but, in this moment, I am supposed to tell you that you have to write a few things down. Really. You must write it down. It goes, 'I am. I will. I want. I have.' Repeat it."

I echoed, **"I am. I will. I want. I have."**

"Great," she said, hugging me. "That's going to help you manifest all your dreams." It was as though we were the only people in the room, in Las Vegas, in the world, in the Universe.

"How do you think I got all this?" she asked, gesturing at the scene. "You're right there. *Just say what you want.* That's all you need to do. You're right there ready to stand out big." Then, she started giving me examples, "I *am* amazing. I *will* give tours of my homes on TV. I *want* to expand my empire. I *have* everything in place to do this."

Then, she looked me in the eyes. "I needed to see you tonight. I needed your energy. You're going to freak out at the opening of the show!" We took a picture and off she went.

My friend and I took our seats and in the very first scene of the show, a giant electrical plug comes out and Katy gets electrocuted. She becomes a singing, swinging, dancing Barbie for the whole concert. Holy cow! I almost fell out of my chair.

When I returned to Naples that Sunday, I set pen to paper and made my I am, I will, I want, I have list.

And, well, here we are. **I AM inspired, I WILL inspire others, I WANT you to be inspired, and I HAVE some inspirational insight to share with you.**

"If you can believe
in something
great, then you
can achieve
something great."

Katy Perry

I am blessed.

I am worthy.

I am loveable.

I am youthful and vibrant.

I am a light.

I am powerful.

I am perfect as I am.

I will surrender and trust.

I will do what needs to be done.

I will leave a strong mark on the world.

I want love with my perfect partner.

I want to build an empire worth millions.

I want to do a national TV segment.

I want to collaborate on a book with Bruce Littlefield.

I have a giving heart.

I have unlimited opportunities for growth.

I have the resources to free my spirit and serve my purpose.

Tiffany
MCQUAID

Insight on INSPIRATION

Here's what I know about inspiration: Finding it, discovering it, spotting it is MY responsibility. It's always been my responsibility, as it is yours. **If you want your life to blossom, then you must encourage that along.** You can't just sit back and wait for it. To be inspired, you must create the conditions to be inspired and then be open to receiving it. I didn't just meet Barbara. I reached out to her. I didn't just open the doors at McQuaid & Company. I worked for it.

You want to eat apples from your own tree? It's not just going to magically appear. It needs nourishment. It starts with a seed, a tiny little kernel. That seed must be planted into soil, preferably some rich soil. Then, it needs light for encouragement, and water and oxygen to combine with that light for energy. With time and care, it will grow, it will blossom, and eventually produce fruit.

The same is true with us. We need a little motivation to blossom and produce fruit. How do we get that inspiration? Sitting on the couch and watching television probably isn't going to do it, even if you're watching the greatest bake off in history or an actor's most legendary performance. Watching other people do something isn't rousing like actually doing it. Inspiration doesn't just walk up behind you and tap you on the shoulder. You must seek it out.

Inspiration has always been my why. I'm a faithful person who (now) believes in signs although this understanding came later in life. I consider these messages from a higher source, and whether you believe in God, Mother Nature, the power of the Universe, or the Great Elf, having faith that there is something bigger than you is powerful. It gives one awe. What I have learned on my journey is that the mental work, strengthening your mind and getting it to a place of understanding that you are not alone, gives you the strength to climb the ladder, and the inner peace to be thoughtful, rather than reactionary, in how you respond to life's circumstances.

Why did Katy Perry's plastic bag speak to me? I had asked for it. I was hungry for it. I had made myself available to it and put myself in the literal path of being open to receiving it.

INQUIRY: What was the last thing that actually inspired you?

I'm always looking for things that move me because I both need to be inspired, and want to inspire others, whether it's my customers or my team. The design of my offices, for example, was inspired by spending the day at Facebook's headquarters in Menlo Park on the edge of San Francisco. Talk about an inspiration tour! Much like how I was transported into Katy's fantastical world of color and vision, I felt a similar electric charge touring Facebook's sprawling campus, which felt more like a town than an office.

In the center of the massive compound are fun places to eat, including an old diner-style restaurant, and other small-town square offerings like an arcade, a dentist, and a barber. Team members ride around campus on branded bicycles, and I watched a small group doing an exercise walk together.

Inside the buildings, their concrete floors are a feature unto themselves, decorated with big vinyl signage that directs walking traffic and indicates spots for selfies and hug circles. The walls showcase giant LED screens, featuring vibrant images, information, and videos, and there are nostalgic items, too, like old record covers and posters. There were snack stations at the end of every hallway offering candy, coffee, and coolers housing all the best cold beverages and an array of waters.

I walked through several of the areas multiple times and each time noticed something different, felt something different. You never know what the mind will connect with and how that might inspire a new concept. My visit to Facebook's campus became an inspirational turning point in the evolution of my own office. Innovation and creativity aren't hatched in a boring, stagnant space. You can invest a boatload of money into the most beautifully designed office, and it might be magazine pretty, a stunning space, but not inspiring. Our brains need stimulation to be forward thinking.

I left Facebook's headquarters with my brain on stimulation overdrive. I had never felt more energized by a space in my life and on the flight home from California, I immediately began redesigning our offices. I wanted color, nostalgia, fun sayings and quotes, video elements, and snacks, lots of snacks. As I thought about my environmental experience, I kept coming back to the word "excited." Anyone who is running a business wants their team and their customers happy and motivated. It's productive to be in a space that raises enthusiasm, encourages optimism, and gives a feeling of warmth and comfort.

I wanted to bring this excitement into our everyday lives right where we work. My goal is that everyone who walks in through our glass doors feels inspired. Our offices are now colorfully decorated with our brand's black-white-and-red color scheme. The flavor is quite different from a typical (boring) commercial space. Our walls are embellished with inspirational quotes, like Einstein's "Creativity is intelligence having fun," and Oprah's "To be successful, be excellent. If you want the best the world has to offer, then offer the world your best!" Ask anyone who works with us. They'll tell you that our space stimulates imagination and activity.

We have individual offices and 11 sections, including the Think Tank, the Beverage Bar, our uber-popular Zen Zone, which has two large massage chairs to help our busy team relax, and the Realtor Store, a menagerie of anything our agents might need to go to the INth Degree for their clients, from red rugs to open house baskets, from shirts to

"Take your inspiration from wherever you find it, no matter how ridiculous."

Roy H. Williams

signage and closing gifts. I converted an old jeweler's safe that was in the space into a broadcast studio, used for recording podcasts, voiceovers, and the ever-present Zoom calls. I'm constantly finding new inspiration and evolving the look to keep it fresh. Right now, I'm planning to install two old-fashioned diner booths and enclose them in glass to create an innovative meeting space. There's also a game area with an old-fashioned arcade style Skee-Ball machine.

The Think Tank is our creative conclave that instigates good thoughts. We go there to brainstorm on our chalkboard calendar wall. The walls feature my early marketing ideas, the so-called "tchotchke mailings," showcased in shadow boxes to inspire employees to think outside the box about marketing and promotion, and a giant giraffe encourages everyone to stand tall above the rest. It's inspired and inspiring.

Looking for your own inspiration for a big idea? Inspiration comes from trying and discovering new things. You can do that in a lot of ways. Some ideas: talking to people, going to a museum, baking a cake, reading a book, watching kids build a sandcastle on the beach, or taking your dog for a walk down a new street.

You can also find a YouTube class on just about anything. Want a few ideas? I'm sure you've heard of TED Talks with energizing people talking about big ideas, but there's also TED-Ed that turns interesting topics into short animations on everything from "Boosting Your Brain Power" to "Why Is Yawning Contagious?" (I'm not going to tell you. Look for yourself!)

Like animation? Check out "Improvement Pill" on YouTube. This channel uses animation to give a quick, multi-vitamin dose of self-improvement and terrific takeaway insight with instruction on topics like "How to Find Your Purpose" and "5 Ideas That Changed My Life."

Want a channel that will give you an emotional high? Try "Mateusz M." Don't you want to find out why Muhammad Ali was the "greatest of all time?" Trust me, you'll finish these videos and be inspired to run a marathon, conquer Mount Everest or, more likely, jumpstart something in your life or business.

If you're wanting some inspiration that will give you a leg up, check out any of Tony Robbins' empowering contributions on the subject. (More on Tony later!) I also watch the MasterClass series on repeat. Advertising executive phenoms Jeff Goodby and Rich Silverstein are two standouts, and I've watched Spanx founder Sara Blakely's class at least six times. I'm moved by her story of trusting that there was something bigger, and that she didn't allow the voices of disbelief or negativity ride along on her journey. She explains that each night at dinner growing up, her dad would ask his kids what they failed at that day. He embraced those shortcomings and empowered them so that they grew up not afraid of failure. Talk about inspiring!

I also just finished Kris Jenner's class which was awesome. Love or hate the Kardashian brand, Kris is an outstanding marketer with some amazing things to teach. She triggered many marketing and promotion ideas for me. I consider it worth my time and attention if I can walk away with at least one nugget of knowledge. Kris's class inspired me to dust off my tap shoes and dare myself to post a "Tapping Tuesday" on social media.

INQUIRY:

Do you watch inspirational YouTube videos and listen to motivational podcasts? Turn off the bad news and put some stimulating immersions on your to-do list.

Let me share my newfound secret about motivation. I'm finding as I get older it seems to be the little things that inspire me the most. Something as seemingly simple (but quite magical) as looking at a flower and realizing that such a beautiful thing forced its way into reality can give me inspiration. I love that! And I crave that. **Inspiration is the key to becoming a successful human, and at the core of becoming a standout for any successful team, organization, or business.** If you are inspired, you are supercharged with enthusiasm and raring to inspire others to be their best selves. If your people are inspired, they are similarly motivated to make your business the best.

Remember your high school football games? I do! One of the credentials on my Life Resume that gave me a lot of joy was my position as a cheerleader. That's right. I was a high school cheerleader and a darn good one, too. It was a thrill cheering for the Falcon football players of Field High School in Brimfield, Ohio. I worked hard on learning my routines so I could get the crowd energized and inspire the team to victory.

Being a cheerleader was an experience that could not have turned out better for my life. I have used that inspirational dynamic so many times in my career, motivating me to keep moving forward, despite the people or circumstances that try to tackle me. The cheerleader in me sparked a natural inclination to root for someone, to encourage them to score in their lives, and to keep them moving forward despite setbacks or hurdles. I'm able to offer support and motivation. This empowers my team and gives them the desire to win.

Want to really step up your inspiration game? Help those around you achieve their goals by being a cheerleader for their skills and capabilities. Think of five people who are important to you, who make a difference in your life and your personal success. Write their names on a piece of paper. Next to each of their names write what you think a goal of theirs might be. Then, think of a way you can help support that goal. It could be as simple as buying them a book on the subject or as easy as spending a lunch talking about their dream. That's how I converted a 15-year-old helper at one of my events into my vice president of operations and a 62-year-old retiree into my go-getter assistant. What does inspiring others to achieve their goals do for you? It builds you up, helps you feel good, and makes you stand out to them!

Cheerleaders might get a cheesy reputation, but trust me, anyone who inspires others to be their best is going to stand out in the crowd, especially if they are doing roundoff back handsprings! Today, the cheerleader in me writes little love notes to my team with each of their commission checks, and often sends them words of encouragement or gives them a hug when I sense they need it. I organize special "delight days" to pull everyone together, give some pats on backs, and create shared, joyful experiences. And, yes, we even have a company "high five!"

Here's a newsflash: As an entrepreneur, no one is going to walk into your office and pop champagne for all you do. No one knocks on my door to say, "Good job, Tiff! Thanks for paying us again this week." You have to figure out how to pop that cork yourself. So, I cheer myself on, literally. And you should figure out a cheer for yourself, too! Before I go on stage to speak or simply need to talk myself into doing something challenging, I always play a little cheer in my head from those days when I wore Falcon red and black. *"L-E-T-S-G-O. LET'S GO, LET'S GO! L-E-T-S-G-O. LET'S GO, LET'S GO!"* I'll do it for you the next time I see you.

Your fourth mission
INVEST IN YOURSELF

MISSION 4

It's time to unlock your brain and stimulate your soul. Let's get you inspired. Put on your headphones or crank up that car stereo and give yourself a "tune up." This investment tune is:

"Firework" by Katy Perry!

Play it a few times while you're on your way to someplace you've never been. Perhaps it's a coffee shop, a bookstore, or an art gallery. Maybe it's a walk with your dog in a new neighborhood or a trip to an arcade. Do something you don't normally do. The goal is to put yourself on the avenue of inspiration. Do it with personality, imagination, enjoyment, and acceptance. Be curious. Let yourself get inspired by everything that surrounds you on the journey: colors, people, smells, sounds, nature. Put your whole spirit into the endeavor and the adventure of it all.

Then, find a nice place to sit and fill in these blanks…

I am _____

I am _____

I am _____

I will _____

I will _____

I will _____

I want _____

I want _____

I want _____

I have _____

I have _____

I have _____

Now, read your list a few times while listening to:
"Simply the Best" by Tina Turner because **YOU are simply the best!**

INGENUITY

KEY 5

THE QUALITY OF BEING CLEVER, ORIGINAL, AND INVENTIVE.

IT'S THE PROBLEM-SOLVING MIRACLE!

When I was young, my grandmother on my dad's side — Grandma Frank as we called her — was super clever and always resourceful. I now realize she was one of my first interactions with someone whose inventiveness helped "get the job done." Her lessons and ingenuity have stuck with me, and I often find myself asking, "What would Grandma Frank do?"

One such story that sticks with me took place one fall when my sister Monica, my cousin Melody and I were all visiting her for the weekend. She had a knack for getting us active and outside, so it was no surprise when she invited us to come to the backyard. There she brought out three different colored rakes and announced a new "game."

Grandma Frank asked each of us to pick a rake, then assigned each of us an area of her backyard. All the leaves had dropped from the trees, and she explained that we were to use the leaves to construct a "playhouse," pulling the leaves together and using our imaginations to shape them into walls, rooms, and furniture. When we were done, she would come back for a tour and announce a winner.

Excitedly the three of us got to raking! We created our wall outlines and fashioned a leaf bed, couch, and chairs. After an hour or so, Grandma Frank came out and announced we had each created a leaf house worthy of *Better Homes & Gardens* and it was simply too difficult to pick a winner. As a reward, she gave each of us a jar of Gerber's vanilla pudding baby food and a tiny spoon so we could eat it right out of the jar. Yum! A personal favorite for all of us!

Then, she asked if we were up for a new game. This one would be timed. We all shouted yes!

Pulling out a stash of big black garbage bags, Grandma Frank asked, "We're going to see who can rake their leaves into these bags the fastest! Ready? Set. Go!" We sprang into action, feverishly raking and bagging, raking and bagging, while scrutinizing each other's progress. Raking and bagging! All while Grandma Frank checked her watch. When every last leaf in her yard was cleaned up, she announced a champion — we'd all taken the prize! She let us each pick from her assortment of small, differently colored Tupperware bowls that she had filled with the Holy Grail of snacks: Double Stuf Oreos.

Through one incredibly inventive (and exhilarating!) exercise, she accomplished her mission. She turned a necessary, mundane task into something delightful for us all. We were thrilled with our fun and none the wiser that we took care of her fall cleanup. **Whether in life or business, finding a creative solution to the challenges always wins the day.** That's ingenuity!

My creative side has always made me a little different and sometimes a party of one. After my dad died, I used my creativity as a distraction from the sad reality that he was no longer in my life. I would deep-dive into my imagination to escape, creating worlds of bliss, a place of my dreams, of stories with happy endings, or I would read books, tons of them, and get lost in those worlds. I took his death very personally and these outlets served as both a reprieve and as a coping mechanism. I would create the world I wanted in my mind's eye and then step into it. Often this would mean I'd spend an afternoon rearranging my bedroom or redecorating the house (typically while my mom

> "Creativity is the power to connect the seemingly unconnected."
>
> William Plomer

was at work or sleeping.) In one legendary exploit, I took all the leftover paint from the garage and repainted my bedroom. I did the basement too, much to my mother's surprise.

In school, I always loved the "project" assignments because they'd ignite my creative brain and allow me to knock it out of the park. I was the kid who looked forward to the annual science fair, not so much for the scientific part, but for the ingenious effort I'd give to the posters, presentation, and competition.

In 6th grade, to showcase the yearly change of the seasons, I disassembled my Mr. Mouth game. Remember the one where a yellow head spun around while players tried to catapult chips into his opening and closing mouth? I wanted to use the spinning base for my wax-paper leaf display. After dismantling the head, I took a white shirt-sized gift box, covered it with construction paper, and attached my leaves to it. I disguised the base with some fall-inspired fabric my mom had stashed in her craft box, and off it spun me to regionals.

"Being different isn't a bad thing. It means you're brave enough to be yourself."

Luna Lovegood,
Harry Potter book series

My attention-getting presentation may not have been stellar science, but my creativity and cleverness got noticed. In fact, the flashy bells-and-whistles of my projects took me to regional competitions several times, including a win for my over-the-top, self-grown crystals and crystalized sign of homemade letters personally decorated with glitter nail polish. It was sparkly!

For each school assignment, I remember thinking, *What can I do that's different? What is going to make my project stand out?*

As I got older, I became my mom's right hand. I had to. She was a single, working mother with two girls, so I often did the cooking, which I loved (still do!), and cleaning. My sister would even pay me to clean her room, so she didn't have to. This responsibility also brought opportunities to be creative. I learned origami so I could fold bath towels into shapes and create cute dinner napkins for the holiday table. Then I became obsessed with nice penmanship and taught myself calligraphy. The formality of that style developed my own "Tiffany style" of writing. I turned my "font" into a moneymaker. In college, I ran an ad in the *Youngstown Vindicator* for "Wedding Invite Calligraphy," charging a quarter per invite. I would write out addresses while working the midnight shift at our local classic rock radio station. Being creative fueled many odd jobs that helped cover my school and living expenses.

I built my real estate business from nothing and have loved every minute of the learning curve. Has everything I created turned into a Rembrandt? No. Sometimes leveraging creativity to grow a business is like throwing a lot of paint at the wall with the results creating more of a Jackson Pollock splatter. The thing about innovation is this: you just have to get your hands dirty. Excitedly immerse yourself in the experience of coming up with new ideas. Step up to the challenge of the unknown and be willing to make a little mess.

Before graphic design programs, I'd gather my materials — from construction paper to photos — and plop down on the floor in front of the TV at night, literally cutting and pasting to design my mailers. I'd make copies and spend another night stuffing and labeling my promotional pieces to go out to my "farm" area. Red became my signature color. I find it a warm, energizing color that excites the emotions and motivates action. I paired it with black because many things I've loved in life have been wrapped in red and black, from my dance costumes to my high school colors. I went through a phase

"Every child is an artist. The problem is staying an artist when you grow up."
Pablo Picasso

90

where all I wore was red lipstick, and now I'm known for my red dresses. Red and black consistently remind me of good things from my past, a friendly tip of the hat to my evolution from yesterday to today. Even now, all McQuaid & Company promotional materials use those colors. The book you're holding is purposefully and boldly red to give you confidence and promote ambition and determination.

Color creates a strong psychological connection and gives incredible power to a brand. The right color combinations should be thoughtfully considered from your logo and advertising to your packaging and website because they can make or break a business. Studies have shown that color influences 85% of a shopper's purchase decision. 85%! That's why there are college courses and numerous psychology studies on color theory.

The color wheel is composed of warm and cool colors. Warm colors, like red, yellow, and orange conjure energy while cool colors like blue, purple, and green induce serenity. Spas pick cool colors to evoke calmness. McDonald's uses red and yellow. Why? Red attracts attention, sparks stimulation, and triggers appetite. Yellow activates the feelings of happiness and friendliness. Combined, the two colors represent speed and quickness. Come in, eat, and head out.

It's important to have an authentic connection to your brand's colors. Whether it was your team's uniform or simply your favorite color, picking a palette from a position of meaning and authenticity will help reinforce your passion for your product, culture, and company moving forward. Most importantly, recognize that people notice and are also affected by the colors you use, so put some ingenuity into the choice because it represents you.

INQUIRY: What is your color? Is it currently part of your business? If you don't have a color, open a box of 64 crayons and see which one (or ones) grab you.

Let's talk about using ingenuity to get noticed. I spend a tremendous amount of time conceiving and designing my advertisements. My mom was a newspaper executive and had access to research for both retail and real estate advertising. When I started in real estate, she shared her knowledge and this advice: "When you run ads in the newspaper, go big or go classified." That little nugget was my point of difference. This trade secret, knowing that smaller ads get lost in the shuffle has helped me place effective ads that get noticed.

For years, I maintained an annual contract with the *Naples Daily News* to run full-page, full-color ads on the back of a main section every Saturday. Why Saturday instead of Sunday you ask? Again, leveraging my mom's wisdom, advertising is about standing out, not blending in. She was absolutely right. At that time, everyone in real estate was putting their money in Sunday's paper. An unexpected ad on Saturday promoting Sunday's open houses got noticed and became my point of difference, one of my secrets to selling success.

Every Saturday morning, I'd go to breakfast at various spots around town to conduct my reconnaissance. I'd sit, sunglasses on, and notice the reactions and behaviors of Saturday morning diners. They'd sip their coffees, nibble their toast, and read the paper. I'd watch when they got to the back of a section to see if they noticed my ad, how long they lingered on it, and if they engaged in dialogue with their companion.

Ingenuity often means taking risks, so sometimes I'd run the ad sideways or upside down to see if that sparked more reaction. Over the years, I've seen an insane number of people at my open houses who I saw the previous day at the diner checking out the ad. Thanks to those attention-getters, and a strategically placed classified ad on Sunday with a spot of color, our open houses stood out among the crowd and were always well attended, leading to great success. Those creative gambles have helped maintain top market share for 21 years. At times, I

"Find what you're good at and use your imagination and creativity at every opportunity."

Richard Branson

represented 90-95% of the active inventory in the community I was marketing.

During my growth, Barbara Corcoran continued mentoring me and offering her often daring ideas. She guided me into an office expansion well before I thought I was ready by saying that I'd kick myself if another tenant moved into the adjacent space. She also advised me to put my face on all my materials including the side of a new McQuaid & Company van. "Tiffany," she explained, "When the other brokerages don't have a face to their name, be sure yours does and plaster it everywhere. People like knowing there is someone accountable when they work with a company." That traveling billboard — which made me super uncomfortable—became well-seen around town.

Ingenuity is thinking through the goal and being clever enough to bring it to life. As my career evolved and my business grew, I closely monitored the reactions and responses to everything I did. From mailers to open houses to showings, always trying to decipher what will elicit the most attention and trigger retention in the minds of the consumer. **If I can impart one piece of money-making wisdom for expanding your business, it's to go all in on ingenuity.** No matter the industry, at some point there's going to be a down market. During that time, if there are any customers out there, you want them! How do you stand out when there are lots of choices? You must use your creativity to design, develop, and craft things that grab attention, and wild ideas often get wild amounts of attention. There are, for example, more than 8,000 realtors in Naples and 200,000 in the state of Florida. If opportunity isn't knocking, it's all about creating opportunity. Build a bigger door and install a doorbell that plays Rachmaninoff!

"Think left and think right and think low and think high. Oh, the thinks you can think up if only you try!"

Dr. Seuss

During the 2020 pandemic, there was a void in the market, a complete absence in clients and prospects. Not even the crickets were chirping! Desperate times called for clever measures. We had to generate our own buzz. Rather than sending out "Just Sold" or "Just Listed" postcards, we created games and other fun activities, such as word searches, coloring contests, and neighborhood scavenger hunts, with the goal of giving people some "feel good" during the difficult times. Our hope was to help break up the monotony of all the isolation.

Our word searches included real estate-related terms and we posted the answer key on our company's social media pages. This sparked larger dialogue and cross-promotional opportunities. In our coloring contest mailer, we encouraged clients to snap a photo of their children's work and text it to us. That served as a jumping off point for communication. When someone submitted an entry, I'd drop off a basket of goodies at their front door. The most important thing during that challenging time was that our company was heart first, giving people something fun to do. It was positive engagement — personal, simple, intimate, and fun — that created an opportunity to continue a conversation. We created a presence when we couldn't be present. The supplemental real estate chat could come later — and it did. We roared out of the pandemic with more than double the business from the same period the previous year.

What's "news?" News is a break in the ordinary. Something that causes a reaction and moves behavior by generating buzz and increased demand. So, if things aren't flowing. What do you do? Innovate! Use your ingenuity to invent something new and newsworthy, proactively creating the outcome you desire... in my case, that's selling a house. In your case, it might be moving merchandise or bringing in more clients.

I had a unique property, unusual in that the owner loved going on safari and had taken many adventures, bringing back trip treasures from every excursion. The entire house was full of those findings, a veritable African museum. There were photos of lions and giraffes, zebra-patterned rugs, tribal relics, and carved figures. Even the placemats were handwoven and unmistakably declared "safari."

The owner wanted to sell this relatively small square-footage property at a price well above the market's top listings. In speaking with her, I explained that getting that price would be a trick and would even set a record sale for the area. We needed to do something that would grab attention, create an organic sense of urgency, and drive many people to the first open house. I had an idea, but it was a wild one. I suggested we lean into her genuine passion about her travels and décor by hosting an open house safari.

She immediately said, "Let's do it!"

My first call was to our local wildlife preserve, Ngala, which stands for "the place of the lion." After attending some of their spectacular events, I became a patron. I reached out to the founder and explained what we were trying to pull off. I asked if they might bring some animals and trainers to the property for two hours on a Sunday afternoon for an open house. To thank them for helping us realize this big dream, I promised to make a nice donation to the wildlife preserve when the house sold. As quickly as you can say "Circle of Life," the deal was done.

We advertised that we had teamed with Ngala to offer the wildest open house in the history of open houses. Everything we sent out was our signature red with splashes of zebra and giraffe prints, setting the stage for what was to come. We created a stunning display. From the moment people arrived, they were engulfed in an unexpected, stunning safari-themed extravaganza.

Our entire team, dressed in safari gear, welcomed more than a hundred visitors, including some who even brought their kids to see the animals. It was breathtaking for people to walk up to this extremely high-priced house and see this jaw-dropper of an experience. An alligator, rescued from a horrid domestic situation, and a beautiful spotted eagle-owl greeted visitors at the front door. When they walked into the house, thanks to specially crafted twelve-foot sliders, the entire space was open and exciting. It felt like something special, an experience. Everyone was taking photos and posting them on social media.

Our seller was a woman in her late seventies who that afternoon was transformed into a giddy schoolgirl. She was effervescent, continuously telling us that it was the best day ever. What made it even better? We sold the house because of that daring event! The buyers saw all the people and felt the need to act fast. To date, our safari house is the second highest price per square foot sale in the community.

When ingenuity leads to daring actions, it is generally delightful for everyone. I can assure you that there's not another realtor in town who would have engaged Ngala and brought their resources to an open house. In fact, some likely whispered I was crazy. What did it do for our business? First, it created a thrilled customer, one who was enthusiastic before, during, and after the sale. Second, we generated great buzz for Ngala and our donation delighted them. Third, we sold the house for top dollar in what was then a transitioning market. But mostly, our imagination created a legendary experience. The larger-than-life safari open house made an impressive impact and created a memorable branding moment for McQuaid & Company. Anyone can slap a sign in the yard and throw some brochures out. What we created was magic. People went away talking about what our company had done. Never underestimate the power of a third-party endorsement for your business. It is priceless.

You've heard the expression "think outside the box." I say, don't think outside the box. Don't think inside the box. Don't even think of the box… unless you're a pizza. But even pizza got creative. Square box, circle pizza, triangle slices. That's both ingenious and memorable. Memorable creates retention. Retention causes top of mind aware-ness, which converts into action. Maybe that's why I'm always ready for pizza! And, perhaps, that's why that product and the companies that sell it, ultimately make a lot of dough!

"You can't wait for inspiration.
You have to go after it with a club."
Jack London

INQUIRY: When visiting a business or dealing with a salesperson, what are the top 3 traits you appreciate?

1. _____

2. _____

3. _____

Now ask yourself, do you and your business present these traits?

Insight on INGENUITY

Marketing, branding, and all the creative oomph that goes along with it is in my DNA. I consider it my superpower. When I'm in creative mode, the ideas come pouring out of me like ticker tape, but creativity is a trait that can be learned. A pianist becomes a pianist by playing. An artist becomes an artist by painting. A baker becomes a baker by throwing some flour around. We become creative by stimulating our imagination and stepping up to the challenge.

I've heard people say they don't have what it takes to be creative. If by "it" they mean the budget, time, resources, product, or team-mates, then I'd say they are stuck in the "box" waiting for someone else to show up with the box cutter. Maybe someone once told them they were wrong for coloring outside the lines. My grandmother always told me to use the lines to my advantage, darken the border around the edges and then shade in the middle. Inevitably, that tech-nique would win the coloring contest, and today with everything I do creatively, I boldly push to the edges or the limits, lightly filling in and layering the details from end-to-end.

Many of us are scared to put our necks out imaginatively because at some point in our lives we were told we were doing it wrong. It happened to me in 4th grade, but I have that experience to thank for helping me crack the code on creative fear and for never again being scared of how others might judge my own inventiveness. Mrs. Koppe was one of my favorite teachers because she was nice and always gave us terrific science projects. One assignment was to combine two related items on oceanography from her list. I chose to create a dictionary of oceanography terms and a fishing game.

The cartoon character Ziggy was popular at the time, and I used this diminutive, bald, barefoot, big-nosed character in scenes paired with various ocean-themed words: Ziggy in a boat, Ziggy riding the back of a whale, Ziggy collecting seashells. You get the idea. My other project was a starfish fishing game. Using a shoebox and paint, I created a body of "water" and fashioned a fishing rod out of a dowel complete with a paperclip hook. Then, I cut lots of small starfish from posterboard. It took forever because I used the "pointillism" technique I'd just learned in art class to detail each leg of the starfish, giving it a realistic effect. Yes, a tad "over the top" compared to the other students' work, but I was proud... until Mrs. Koppe made each of us get up in front of the class and share our projects. When my turn came, I completely froze under the critical glare and snickers from the mean girls in my class. Self-conscious tears streamed down my face.

At the end of class, Mrs. Koppe asked me to stay after. What she told me has reverberated in my soul ever since. "Tiffany," she said, "You had the best project, but you ruined it because you started crying. Don't ever let other people make you feel bad for being imaginative. Being original is a gift. Never forget that."

A few months later, it was time for the school Spelling Bee. I loved this event as I prided myself on writing and spelling. The entire school gathered in the cafeteria to watch as the school's best spellers vied for the championship. I took my place in line with the other finalists, standing next to Mrs. Lentz, the teacher who would give the cue that it was our turn to step up. She whispered to me, "You're not going to cry, are you?" It was a punch. Mrs. Koppe had obviously told her about my episode. Instead of crumbling, it steeled my spine. I was going to S-H-I-N-E.

"Don't think. Thinking is the enemy of creativity. It's self-conscious and anything self-conscious is lousy. You can't try to do things. You simply must do things."

Ray Bradbury

I took to the stage and, once again, saw dirty looks from that same set of girls. The difference was I had Mrs. Koppe's words buzzing in my head. I moved forward in the bee until I was one of the final two. My knockout word was, ironically, "INtuitive." I had not heard the word before but sounded it out: "I-N-T-U-A-T-I-V-E." Whammy! I finished as the runner up and won a paperback *Webster's Dictionary*, but the real win was that I had the satisfaction of not letting judgment kick me in the teeth. I stood strong. **Being original is a gift. Never forget that.**

Creativity often needs a little encouragement. When my team is working on a project, I often invite them to my house to bang out ideas over homemade banana bread and coffee. Other times we talk ideas through while we nosh over a meal at a favorite restaurant by the beach. We also brainstorm sitting in our massage chairs or scheme up new marketing concepts and strategies while playing a game of Skee-Ball.

When we're outside of the office playing, people loosen up and become extra engaging, brainstorm-y, and problem solving. Yet another tip from Barbara Corcoran that has proven true. Everyone is open, willing to offer new ideas, and more eager to consider the myriad of possibilities. When we move beyond our norm, we always land on genius ideas. Changing the scenery helps get us out of our heads and we have a ball doing it together.

Recently, we were up for a new construction project named "The Grove" in a budding area of Naples called Bayshore. We were up against three big companies, as well as the prospect of the developer potentially manning the sales center themselves and just outsourcing the marketing component. We immediately launched a collaborative team brainstorm session focused on what we could do to knock their socks off. We dove into research about that area, devoured information we were given about the development, and developed concepts that — with our participation — we felt were certain to lead to success.

One of the development's standout features is that it will be located next to where the National Pickleball Championships are held. Knowing that pickleball players will create a pool of potential clients, we wanted to show Mike and Jerry, the dynamic developer duo, that we not only understood their concept, but we could also serve them in a way that betters everyone's chances to score.

I always tell my team to figure out what the baseline of doing something is and know that's what most of our competition will offer. Then, think about how we can kick it up 10 or 20 notches. Ingenuity doesn't have to be complicated. It's just giving a little more thoughtful effort. The extra mile is never crowded.

We asked ourselves, what's something that is going to surprise and delight them? I thought of the golfers swinging their clubs in my backyard and asked, "What are the rules and tools of pickleball?"

It was our "Aha!" moment.

We showed up for the meeting, raring to go. We were the last ones to present, which I always feel is a lucky position, and slammed it over the net. The developers had given each real estate firm the same data, blueprints of the development, and floor plans. We weren't surprised to find out that the other companies showed up and presented baseline motions, with generic collateral and minimal creative inspiration. One did have a personal video message from the president of their company who couldn't be there in person.

When the developer's team walked into the room for our presentation, gifts were waiting for each of them — custom pickleball cases emblazoned with The Grove logo we'd created featuring a juicy Florida orange, branded pickleball paddles, and, consistent to our orange theme, orange pickleballs. They were blown away. We presented two logo options, both of which they loved, and converted their blueprints into full-color renderings with sexy, 3D images of the development's exterior. After we left, orange Bundt cakes were delivered with a thank you note for meeting with us.

Want to know what happened?

Drumroll please...

We got the development, which will generate millions of dollars in commissions for us! Planning and resourcefulness paid off! Further, to give my team a key connection point with what we believe will be a potential customer base for this project, I signed the entire company up for private pickleball lessons. We're going to have an immersive understanding of the game, which I'm betting will give us a competitive edge in the ability to convert lookers into buyers.

Trust me when I say your competition will typically present the status quo business presentation. **If you want to stand out, go all in and give a creative WOW.** Ingenuity for the win!

"Ingenuity is the ability to create something new and useful out of the materials and tools at hand."

Thomas Edison

Ingenuity can also be used to save money. Our office was originally on the smaller size, but with Barbara's advice I expanded into the adjacent space, spreading us into about 5,000 square feet before we had the furniture or the people to fill it. Yes, it was a big risk to expand before we were ready, especially when finances were tight, but the flipside of that frightened thinking is that I was setting my company up for future growth. It was a leap of faith, but I had a vision in my head for how I wanted it to look — a fantastical, Katy Perry inspired space, right down to the quotes on the walls and the fonts used to inscribe them. I got creative and went "treasure hunting" to find pieces and décor that would fit my vision. I found office furniture on Craigslist, purchased light fixtures on clearance, and engaged a local sign company to create impactful imagery.

We managed to piece together something on a dime that still causes "oohs" when people walk in for the first time. It's such a hit that one of our local business journals did a feature story on our office design, proclaiming our space to be "trendy and unique."

INQUIRY: Does your work environment inspire creativity?

Ingenuity is the ability to come up with new ideas and solutions to problems. It is essential for businesses to be successful in today's ever-changing world.

Ingenuity is Ben Franklin standing in a thunderstorm with a kite and a key.

Ingenuity is Wilbur Wright running beside his brother Orville as he took flight on a beach at Kitty Hawk.

Ingenuity is Thomas Edison saying "Aha!" as he passed current through a little filament in his lightbulb.

Ingenuity is hosting an open house safari to attract attention in a transitioning market.

Ingenuity is creating paddleball kits for developers who are building a community next to the National Pickleball facility.

Ingenuity is making our mailers as big as the post office allows. (That's 12 x 15 inches, and a bonus is the mail carrier wraps our smiling faces around the other mail before stuffing it in the box.)

Ingenuity is rolling out a red (branded!) carpet at the entry to our business and at our open house locations.

Ingenuity is going back-to-basics to stand out by sending hand-written notes, rather than a follow-up email, whenever possible. Even picking up the phone or having a cup of coffee together can be radically innovative in today's techno world.

Ingenuity is building relationships with your customer base that are more than transactional. Ones that are respectful, thoughtful, and that show they are valued. Acknowledging life milestones or a "just thinking of you" note let's people know they have a special place in your head, your business, and, if they are lucky, in your heart.

Ingenuity understands that the greatest opportunity to grow and evolve your business comes when you position yourself outside the "norm" for your industry. Purposefully look for other avenues other than what's expected to showcase yourself and what you offer. For example, you will stand out more if you open your physician practice anchoring a small strip plaza than in a professional center or a building surrounded by similar practitioners. An ear doctor will find success sponsoring or marketing at a concert. A foot doctor would be clever to support a walk-a-thon. The most important thing about ingenuity is to find the thing that will make what you're offering stand out. Look for a great "tie-in" to grab the consumer and cleverly create retention.

Don't second guess or give up on creativity. Keep at it. Be willing to color outside the lines and eventually an amazing idea will blossom. As a bonus, allowing your imagination to play will keep you young. Seriously, when was the last time you let your imagination run wild? Today is the day! One of the best ways to be ingenious is to simply be open to new ideas by being willing to try some crazy things on for size. Experiment! Play! How can you flip something in your business? Don't worry if mistakes are made or you spill a little paint. Don't listen to those who say you're crazy! Keep on going! Be passionate. And invite others to join your party.

Need some creative inspiration to get going? Read Dr. Seuss. Watch a centipede take a walk. Pick a different route to work. Lip-sync to the number one selling album on the charts. Go to the zoo and watch the monkeys. Take a test drive in a convertible. Google "most fun restaurant" and invite a friend to join you there for dinner. Put on your PJs, play your favorite song, and dance! I've never had a bad thought while dancing.

Challenge yourself to find where your inspiration can bloom. The most important thing to ingenuity is to get out of your head and dare to dream!

"Creativity is a wild mind and a disciplined eye."

Dorothy Parker

INVEST IN YOURSELF

MISSION 5

It's time to expand your life and business by encouraging your creativity, finding your point of difference, and leveling up. Ready to arouse some inventiveness? Let's add *Over the Rainbow/Wonderful World* by Robin Schulz, Alle Farben, and Israel Kamakawiwo'ole to our playlist. See the skies of blue and the clouds of white! And think to yourself what wonderful things you have to offer!

After you give that a listen or two, let's look for some "Shiny Pennies." What are Shiny Pennies? Grab a handful of pennies and place them on the table. Most will be dull and filthy. But the clean, shiny one will immediately stand out. It gets noticed. Shiny Pennies for your business are the things that make you, your product, your service, or your role in your company stand out. **What are the top five things that make your business shine?**

1.

2.

3.

4.

5.

Knowing these things will allow you to zag, while others are zigging.

How can you cleverly use what you know to get attention and create top of mind awareness?

Think of some things that you love:

Color: _____

_____

Word(s): _____

_____

Number: _____

_____

Symbol: _____

_____

Song: _____

_____

Animal: _____

_____

Activity: _____

_____

Place: _____

_____

Person: _____

_____

Now, use this list as jumping off "passion points" to create next-level wows for you and your company. You will quickly find these can become Shiny Pennies. Here's my list, and how I've used my favorites. It makes "cents!"

Color   Red! It's the featured color on all our collateral materials, in our office décor, and as a backdrop on my Zoom calls.

Word   "Peace." I just cleverly used it as the key word in a new listing: "Make this little PEACE of Quail Creek yours!"

Number   22! It's unity, harmony, and teamwork. When I see the number, I use it as my guide to know the Universe is telling me I'm on the right path.

Symbol	A feather. When I find one, it's validation to me that the brainstorm I'm thinking of is the one that's going to lead to the biggest rainbow.
Song	"Roar" by Katy Perry. I play it anytime I need a quick pick-me-up, and it's my "walk out" song for every speaking or sales event.
Animal	Penny! My long-haired Dachshund. I use her as my reminder to have fun and always look for life's shiny pennies.
Activity	Getting a massage. I use the time on the table to let my brain relax and inevitably I walk out of there with a big idea hopping in my head.
Place	Naples, of course! But how about running a contest in your office and sending the person who has sold the most to your favorite restaurant, your favorite spa, or your favorite resort? There's nothing like a dangling carrot to inspire ingenuity!
Person	My mom. Her words of wisdom are a part of every McQuaid & Company advertisement: Go BIG or go classified.

What are you selling?

Use your creativity and your favorite things to promote it!

INCENTIVE

KEY 6

*A THING THAT MOTIVATES OR ENCOURAGES
ONE TO DO SOMETHING.*

IT'S WHAT MAKES ALL OF US TICK.

I started my first money-making venture the summer I was twelve years old. We didn't have a corner store where I lived in rural Ohio or any place that offered sweet treats other than the rare visit from the ice cream man. I saw an opportunity knocking. I decided to take the Little Debbie Oatmeal Creme Pies my mom would buy for us during her Saturday grocery store excursions and sell them on Monday when she went to work. My store was a rather simple front yard set-up consisting of a card table, a custom handmade sign, a pile of snack cakes, and a pitcher of ice-cold Kool-Aid. Back then, the Creme Pies were around 75 cents for a box of 12 individually wrapped treats, and I would sell one for a quarter. Add that to my quarter-a-cup Kool-Aid, I was making bank.

My summer entrepreneurial gig went well until my mom discovered a stash of the snack cakes while putting clothes away in my sister's drawers. She asked my sister why she was hoarding them, and her honest response was "because Tiff sells them every Monday to the neighbor kids." Mom was mad, grounding me "for life" and making me reimburse her for all the boxes sold. The minor victory for my little entrepreneurial heart — I got to keep the profits.

My mom's exasperated declaration was: "None of my card club friends' kids do things like this." The subtext was why couldn't I just fit in and be "normal" like the rest of the kids. Normal has never been in my DNA. My mind has always been on overdrive, eternally looking for an opportunity to do something unexpected. My actions weren't bad. They just weren't kid typical, and as a child, that sometimes got me into trouble. As an adult, it's helped me stand out and succeed.

Looking back on my Little Debbie front-yard store, I realize my incentive wasn't money. Besides being exciting and fun, I got great satisfaction from pulling in customers, the exhilaration of making a sale, and the joy of seeing their delight. My short-lived entrepreneurial gig provided a point of difference and allowed me to connect and socialize with neighborhood kids. The extra cash was nice, but the planning, set-up, and sales gave me a sense of purpose. Making the other kids happy made me happy. That was the real payoff.

From the moment we are born, we quickly learn about incentive. We wriggle and squirm; someone calms us down. We cry out; someone feeds us. We behave; we get special treats.

When I was a toddler beginning my potty-training journey, my mom said she struggled to find an incentive that would get me out of my diaper and into big girl panties. A popsicle finally worked. Let's call that what it was: a bribe. Every time I did the right thing, I got a popsicle. I learned quickly. Action followed by reward. What my mom didn't anticipate was that I would request a popsicle almost every time I came out of the bathroom for the next few years!

The incentive for reward continued. I didn't want to miss school because I wanted to get the "perfect attendance award." I kept my room clean to get my allowance. I'd do extra things around the house, so I could go to my friends' slumber parties. I'd give extra effort on homework for a sticky metallic star at the top of the paper or, even more enticing, one of the scratch-and-sniff stickers. (Remember those!?)

"Making money is a happiness. And that's a great incentive. Making other people happy is a super-happiness."

Muhammad Yunus

I was a latchkey kid. My mom worked every day and, as the oldest, I was responsible for getting my sister and me home from school safely. I took my role and the chores I was given very seriously. Why? Because my mom trusted me with caring for her precious goods (us!) and tackling tasks to help maintain the household. I was enticed with an allowance, but the more valued reward was seeing joy on my mom's face when she came home to a clean house and washed dishes. That was my motivation. Seeing her happy made me happy and encouraged me to do more. I started cooking and doing the laundry. She didn't ask me to do this. I did it because it felt good. The satisfaction of a job well done was irresistible and helped sweeten my financial reward of $2.00 per week, but the best "dangling carrot" was my mom's smile. It warmed my heart and was the reason I took on more and more. That's an incentive.

INQUIRY: What's something extra you do in your tasks at home or work that makes you extra happy?

Whether we realize it or not, incentives touch our lives daily. As entrepreneurs, we often forget that motivation should be a core tenet in our business plans. From staff to clients, everyone not just likes, but needs, enticements to work hard as an employee or to buy what you're selling as a customer.

Financial reward is why most of us take jobs. We must make money to afford our lives and provide for our families. Once we take that job, we need incentives to help us stick with it and to help keep us satisfied. Motivation is something that creates warm fuzzies, which could be extra vacation days, titles and awards, or praise and accolades.

Let me tell you about my core team and what I found motivates them.

I met Helen during the second listing I ever had. I was new to real estate and was visiting an upcoming property to give it some needed sprucing up. It had been on the market with another agent to no success because, in my opinion, it lacked personality and flow. The sellers were mostly living out of the country, and the house appeared vacant. My mission was to add some character and make it feel lived in. When I arrived to begin my styling, I punched in the home alarm's security code, and the system began screeching loudly. No matter what I tried, I couldn't get it to shut off, and I knew I was in trouble.

A few minutes into the shrill squawking, a beige station wagon whipped into the driveway and out popped a petite, blond-haired, barefoot lady who came barreling toward me. "What did you do?" she asked, as she bounded past me to enter the code. When all was finally quiet, I introduced myself and told her I was the new real estate agent for the listing. She shook my hand and said, "I'm Helen, the home check person." The sellers had spoken fondly of her. I explained I was bringing in some things to "set the stage" for showing with hopes of securing a sale. She nodded approvingly.

A few days later when Helen came to do her check, I was in the house doing some staging magic. "Wow," she said, looking around the house. "This looks so much better. I'm so glad you're doing this. I can tell you really care." Little did I know how much I would come to care for her, too.

The house sold fast, and I didn't see Helen again until a couple of years later. I bumped into her while out in Naples where she explained that she was no longer checking homes because a personal health issue had changed her course. She said she was hoping to find a part-time job with lots of flexibility, and I immediately offered her a position as my assistant, not knowing what I would have for her to do or what I'd pay her. I'd never had a direct employee of my own before, and the lay of the land wasn't yet mapped. "How about we start with 10 hours a week and see what happens?" I remember telling her.

"I don't use a computer," she said, emphatically. I didn't blink because I remembered the way she cared for the home I was selling. I was carrying 24-28 listings in my community by myself and needed some help, even if I didn't know what kind. Three months later, Helen was working full-time for me and became a vital part of my company's growth. Throughout our run, Helen never used a computer — for anything. She picked up the phone and spoke to people, and the personal relationships she developed helped my business grow. She was by my side as I made the transition to my own office. She developed a rapport with every vendor and became a much-liked liaison with my buyers and sellers.

What was Helen's incentive for all her dedication? Helen wanted to feel needed and appreciated. And that she was! For 12 years, Helen was my backbone, my pusher, my personal encourager, and the office get-it-doner. Time and time again, her personal communication with others saved the day. There were several tough spells where her relationships with our creditors literally kept the lights on. Quite simply, Helen was and remains a blessing. Without her, I don't know how I would have done it. She was my human "Shiny Penny," a dear, valued, respected, cherished, bright spot in our office.

Although she retired from her office duties, she's still a vital part of my life and is always looking out for me. As we like to joke, she's now become my furry friend Penny's assistant. It's more like a shared custody arrangement. She picks Penny up every morning during the week and drops her back each afternoon, so Penny is waiting to greet me at the door. Penny has given Helen, now in her 80's, a purpose, an incentive to keep going, and the relationship has truly allowed her to continue to shine.

Another one of my stars is Nicholas, our Vice President of Operations. We met when he was 15 years old working on an event together. He's wise beyond his years and always carried himself with an air of responsibility, so I had no idea he was that young. It wasn't until the end of the event when someone shared his inability to drive a car that I discovered his age.

A few years later, our paths crossed again while working on some events in Downtown Naples, and I offered Nicholas a part-time position. It was going to be a jaunt since he lived in Fort Myers, but at least then he was old enough to drive.

"Work gives you meaning and purpose, and life is empty without it."

Stephen Hawking

He started working in our office after school. One day, when Nicholas was a high school senior, he showed up at my office door and asked if we could talk.

Nicholas said he wanted to be at McQuaid & Company full-time and his intention was to drop out of school and complete his GED on the side. I nearly fell out of my chair, and asked, "Have you spoken to your mother about this?"

"Not yet," he said. I suggested he have the discussion with his mom, not me, but that he'd always have a home in our company.

The next thing I knew, Nicholas was coming to the office full-time and walked across the stage to graduate with his class. Mind-boggling for sure, but there was no doubt that he was motivated. What was important to Nicholas was that someone recognized his gifts and his vision. He's played a pivotal role in our company ever since. What continues to be his incentive? He loves being appreciated. There's nothing like his smile when I tell him "attaboy."

I met Adam, our Vice President of Creative, when he was working at a printing vendor I used. Adam was always enjoyable to work with and recognized that my concepts on printed materials were "outside" of what was normal in our industry. I was always trying new, crazy things, and he was always encouraging of the designs and used his skills to realize my vision.

After a few years, I realized his Technicolor brain was a perfect fit to start our in-house promotional division. His incentive? He wanted the opportunity to grow and the freedom to create. Together, we have magnetic synergy. I can have a concept, and, with brief expla-nation, Adam can read my mind and bring it to life in the most incredible way. Allowing his imagination to blossom has made inno-vative magic for our firm.

Nicole, our Vice President of Marketing, was working for a local public relations company we were using. I've never been one for resumes, preferring to notice people's actions, and I observed that Nicole would sit quietly in meetings, taking it all in, and then magically whip out terrific observations and ideas. She got it and that got me, plus her nurturing vibe was nice to be around. Although that initial stint together was brief, I never forgot her manner and kept her contact information on my desk. A few years later, I asked her if she'd assist us part-time with some marketing. She came aboard and immediately began offering great suggestions.

During the pandemic, even though the timing was not the best from a financial perspective, it became clear to me that bringing her on full-time was the ideal next step. I hired her and knew I'd figure out the rest. Nicole's primary incentive was her well-defined desire to be a mother and have a family. Having a job that would allow her that flexibility was one of her crucial job requirements. We have been blessed to evolve through that journey with her. We hosted an "About to Pop" popcorn-themed baby shower for her and were thrilled when she had the "first baby of McQuaid." Watching her motherhood journey has been special, and for us, her nurturing and protective nature is an asset that we all appreciate and need.

Krista, our Vice President of Communications, left a 25-year career in broadcasting to accept a position on our team. We became friends hosting area events, as both she and I share the joy that comes from creative expression. After years of anchoring the nightly newscast and carrying the weight of all that bad news, she decided it was time to explore other ways to use her talents. One morning, I woke up to a Facebook message asking if I knew anyone who would or could use her skillset. I wrote back, "Yes... US!" I had been thinking for a few months about how to incorporate more video into our business but didn't know exactly how to accomplish that.

Krista was the missing piece. Her creative experience is a natural fit for our company, and her fresh approach has helped open the door to new things. Her incentive for this career move? She needed a change, wanted the chance to be creative, and dreamed of a more normal schedule.

And what's my motivation? Why do I work so hard? The incentive for me today is the same as it was back when I set up my Little Debbie stand. It makes me happy to make other people happy. Back then, my incentive was to create a spot in rural Ohio where the neighborhood kids could come, get a treat, and hang out. I now know that joy for me comes from creating something from nothing and in creating special moments for others. Yes, I love making money, and money is certainly necessary to buy both necessities and luxuries, but there's another incentive for doing what I do. My work gives me validation. I love the sense of accomplishment I get from contributing to the big dreams of others.

Now, let's talk about incentives for customers and clients to use your services and buy your products. **Why should people invest in what you're selling? What enticements do you offer?**

Remember Trick or Treating as a child? I can still picture the houses of neighbors who gave out the Holy Grail of treats — full-size candy bars. My friends and I would label the standouts with monikers like "The Snickers" house or "The M&M's guy." (We had a neighbor who worked for M&M's world-famous confectionary Mars, Inc. and his house was always our first stop.) The point is we never forgot who had the good stuff, where they lived, and the excitement we felt. When you're operating a business, you want customers to remember you and that can start with a lure, but the enticement is really what goods or services you're offering and whether you're hooking the client once the bait is set.

One of my early adult jobs was working on marketing and events for a national shopping center developer. In a constant effort to bring traffic to the mall, we hosted events almost every weekend, from arts and craft fairs to car shows, from senior health and wellness expos to concerts. Organizing, planning, and managing these happenings always gave me an adrenaline rush. It was a powerful learning experience that created an invaluable arsenal of knowledge for my current business.

An event like a senior health and wellness expo would typically be sponsored by a local hospital or healthcare facility and could attract thousands of people. There would be featured speakers, health testing and wellness checks, and lots of vendors that cater to and target that demographic. It presented an incredible opportunity for businesses to connect directly with potential new customers if they planned thoughtfully.

Inevitably, attendees would go from booth-to-booth collecting a wide selection of goodies like a branded nail file, letter opener, or stress ball in their complimentary "swag" bags. Many visitors were like trick or treaters just walking from booth to booth to gather freebie souvenirs, while not really digesting the nature of the business. That is not the intent of these types of shows, nor the result of marketing or advertising money being well spent. The idea is to lure people in with incentives such that you can cultivate a relationship, create a customer, and lay the groundwork for future business. The freebie should be a result of engagement, not just a "here ya go."

"So, speak up, America. Speak up for the home of the brave. Speak up for the land of the free gift with purchase."

Elle Woods,
Legally Blonde 2

A booth staffed with people sitting in chairs, not making eye contact, and waiting for attendees to come by, might give away a lot of freebies, but that enterprise is not going to gain many new customers. The booth that is staffed by energetic, smiling people who are on their feet and saying "hello" to passersby gives the incentive for conversation and that starts the act of conversion, persuading an attendee to become a customer. The giveaway should be the cherry on top of a delicious presentation and engagement already made or had.

The booths at the Expos that were stand-outs were notable for their unique setups and their dynamic salespeople, as much as their takeaway. For example, Estée Lauder erected mirrors, which showed attendees how their skin would look as it aged without their product. Yes, they gave away samples of anti-aging serums, but they gained hundreds of customers. No one wanted to look like they did in those mirrors! I also remember the owner of a therapeutic massage business who always requested the end of a row of booths where he set up massage chairs and gave a five-minute neck rub. He always had a line waiting for his handiwork. His giveaway? A free 15 minute add on coupon for any client that scheduled a 45 minute in office massage. It was no surprise that this became the busiest massage office in town.

Treats cause retention, whether a potty-training popsicle, a letter opener, or a full-size candy bar, but the incredibly powerful lesson is they bring business when they are paired with positive engagement or further benefit to the recipient.

Gift with purchase, anyone? Clinique created an empire by incentivizing customers by offering a free gift with purchase. Spend $30 and get a travel bag! Or buy perfume, get the atomizer for free! It's a lure, dangling bait. My mom would wait to buy her favorite Clinique lipstick until the perfect promotional item was offered. Successful gift-with-purchase promotions generate strong emotions and brand loyalty, and often get a consumer to try a product they wouldn't have. The feeling of getting something for FREE is a stimulant, and marketing experts will tell you the word "free" comes only behind the words "you" and "yours" in creating a draw. That's incentive in action.

Whether it's showing houses or visiting the dentist, the ones that are remembered and favored are the ones that offer the extra something. At an open house, the enticement might be walking away with one of our delicious individually wrapped Bundt cakes. At the dentist, it might be the take-home toothbrush kit. At the nail salon, it might be the shoulder rub or the sample size of sumptuous hand lotion you're gifted. The connection comes in that someone has given thought, gone all in on extra steps to stand out, to be remarkable, and for that extra effort, they are remembered.

I've mentioned my "surprise and delights" before, from sending bouquets of flowers and pizzas to branding pickleball paddles with a developer's logo, but now let me underline the importance by sharing that there's science behind it. When you surprise someone with something special, you activate the frontal cortex of the brain so that interaction becomes more memorable. You physically create a sweet spot that makes your business stand out. It's magical.

While working on this book, we've made reconnaissance trips to various businesses to note what they do to spur interest in their goods or services. Quite frankly, some businesses fail to give any substantive reason at all. One such example is what I'll call "the rock store," a business in the fancy part of town that specializes in pricy geodes, crystals, and organic materials for home décor. We walked in and began browsing. No one greeted us. We began admiring their wares, turning over a few price tags, and commenting on how we might find a place for this or that piece somewhere in our homes.

INQUIRY: What is your company's "gift with purchase?" What are you doing, offering, or giving that elevates you or your business to leave someone with a good feeling?

We didn't encounter their two salespeople until we were in the back of the store. One was sitting behind a desk. The other was propped on a petrified wood stump, which I'm sure was expensive. "Hot day," the stump sitter said, while the one behind the desk sipped on her bottle of water.

"Sure is," I said, looking at a sparkly rock with a $4,000 price tag.

That was the conversation in its entirety. Two words from her and two words from me. There was no further anything. Even if I'd fallen in love with that $4,000 glittery nugget, I wouldn't have bought it. The non-dynamic duo was actually a disincentive. I would have always looked at my rock and thought "hot day," rather than admire its twinkle.

Let's envision a different scenario, an INth Degree one, where the staff had an incentive to sell us a dream. Imagine the contrast had we been greeted at the door and pointed to a few items of interest in the store. Or fancy if you will, rather than sitting behind a desk drinking a bottle of water on that hot day, the salesperson offered us a chilled bottle of water or a glass of bubbly to cool us off while we shopped. Picture one of them telling us a story about an item we'd shown interest in: "Isn't that incredible?" she could have asked. "That's an extremely rare, 160-million-year-old amethyst found deep in the Rio Grande do Sul region of Brazil." What if they had invited us to an upcoming geode-opening demonstration the store was having? (There's a free idea for you, Rock Store people. I'm betting it would draw a rocking crowd.)

It's a stone-cold fact that they gave us absolutely no reason, no incentive, to buy anything they were selling.

 **INQUIRY:** Think of one of your favorite businesses. Why is it your favorite? What elements do they offer to maintain your loyalty?

During our INvestigations, I had two friends from out-of-town pose as a couple looking to buy a house and visit the offices of some of my real estate competitors. In one, someone yelled from a back office, "let me know if you have any questions," but didn't get up. My friends walked into another storefront and described it as "crickets." No music, no people, no nothing, only some scattered brochures and promotional materials on a table by the front door. At one fancy agency, they were greeted at the door with a smile, offered a bottle of water, and then abruptly asked, "What's your budget?" They said it felt like a first date wanting to get you home rather than get to know you.

There was one office where they came away impressed, despite the unimpressive storefront with listings printed out on regular copy paper and taped to the window. When they entered, a young man sitting on a folding chair right inside the door stood up and said, "Hi! I'm Jack. How may I help you today?" My friends explained they were visiting Naples and just being nosy about the real estate market. Jack explained there was a lot to love about Naples, bragging about our gorgeous white sand beaches and touting that Naples ranks as one of the "best places to retire in the United States." Quickly adding, "Not that you look like you're old enough to retire anytime soon." He said there were properties of all price ranges to suit every need, and then pointed out two of his favorite properties currently on the market, one that was $600,000 and one that was $1.7 million. He noted the attributes of both.

My friends said they weren't ready to buy, but they were really liking the scene. He said, "Me too. I love it here." He pulled out his card which, like the featured window listings, had been printed and hand cut from a piece of regular office paper. "This is actually my uncle's firm," he explained. "I just finished college and came down from Jacksonville to get started in real estate. When you're ready to start looking, I'm happy to help." Of the offices they visited, Jack was the one they would have chosen for their agent. Why would they pick the newbie? He was personable, honest, and eager. They thought it would be an enjoyable experience to go out and look at homes with him. These

"Motivation is the art of getting people to do what you want them to do because they want to do it.

Dwight D. Eisenhower

qualities and his willingness to share his favorite properties won the vote on who my friends would select as their agent. He was likable and gave them warm fuzzy incentives.

Yesterday, I saw my favorite bagger at my much-loved farmstand. I was on my way to a big pitch and wanted to bring along some flowers and cookies for my potential clients. I walked up to the register and said, "Lucky me! It's you!"

"I haven't seen you in forever," she said. "Well, there you are!" I said. "The best bagger in the history of baggers." "You have no idea how I needed to hear something nice today," she said. "I haven't been here in a while because I've been dealing with some things, and you've given me the right start on my first day back. Thank you so much." "Thank you!" I told her. "It's always a great day to see you." I left with my flowers, cookies, and a smile on my face. **A pleasant encounter is food for the soul and an incentive to return to a business again and again.** As I drove out of the parking lot, I realized words of affirmation are a sprinkle of fairy dust. The incentive is kindness. It's caring. It's smiling. It's giving someone a hug. It's acknowledging a job well done. It's as simple as that. We all want to be seen, heard, and feel like our day has worth.

The flowers and cookies from the farmstand were for clients that had been referred to us on Sanibel Island. On the way to that big pitch, I stopped by the office to pick up Krista, our Vice President of

Communication, and wrap the cookies in some tissue and put them in a gift bag. Anyone can give a plastic tub of cookies, but making it pretty takes a little extra thought and adds a special touch. There was a decorative butterfly in the flower arrangement, and among the many gift bags in our supply closet, I found one with beautiful butterflies all over it. I wrapped up the cookies and Krista and I headed to the Sanibel property for our big pitch, both feeling like we could conquer the world. We walked into the house with our cookies and flowers for what was our second visit to present our marketing and pricing report. After our hellos, I gave our gifts to the wife. "This is so beautifully wrapped," she immediately noted. "How did you know I love butterflies?"

Imagine my surprise when her husband said, "Butterflies and cardinals. Butterflies and cardinals. Those are her two favorite things."

"Cardinals?" I asked. "Cardinals are my sign from my mom! Every time I see one, I think of her and my heart smiles. She loved them."

It was an instant connection! In that moment, I knew I was meant to be there and meant to help them with their property. That moment set the stage for a great day. After touring the house again, we sat down to discuss how we'd price and market the property. I told them their house was indeed special, noting its specific attributes. It was such an extraordinary home. It had welcomed several presidential visits, and was secure enough to survive the fiercest of storms with only 35 roof tiles missing after Hurricane Ian. The custom-made, million-dollar windows were engineered to handle up to 220 mile per hour winds, making it a virtual Fort Knox. In addition, the distinctive home sits on two combined parcels with an incredibly rare 700 feet of private beach frontage. When I set the price, I knew all of that made for not only a great story, but also a big incentive to any buyer!

"I want to tell you that we've met with everybody, every big realtor in town," the husband began. "There were some heavy hitters in the bunch, but no one has been as thoughtful as you. After our last meeting, your presence was felt even after you left." This is a man who has been extremely successful, written numerous books, and been awarded Presidential honors. "You noted attributes about our property that no one else did. You see the things here that make you inclined to take some risks. That's all great, but really here's why we're going to give you the listing: The most important thing is that both of us feel a connection with you that we didn't feel with anyone else."

That's incentive. And, my friends, is the big secret of sales.

It's not just people doing business. It's people having a relationship. It might just be selling a simple Little Debbie snack cake, but if you create a moment for someone that spurs a smile, a conversation, a connection, you can put a "SOLD" sign on whatever you're offering.

"Act as if what you do makes a difference. It does."

William James

Insight on INCENTIVE

What incentive does someone have to choose you over your competition? What are you doing to lure them in? How are you brightening their day? Why will they remember you? What does it look like when someone walks into your establishment? Is it inviting? Friendly? Happy? If we want to be successful, we should consistently elevate the experience for those we encounter. This attracts people to you and what you're selling like bees to a flower.

Have you ever gone to a clothing shop or hair salon that offered you sparkling water or a glass of champagne? What does it encourage you to do? Shop! Get comfortable! What happens at that moment? It elevates perception of value. It says, this isn't an ordinary, run-of-the-mill, this is an experience. And we all buy into a nice experience.

When someone walks into McQuaid & Company, they are right away greeted warmly by someone and offered a beverage. They also immediately see our front credenza which is filled with jars of nostalgic candy. This makes a statement that you are welcome here, and your time with us is going to be a delight. Several months ago, a couple came in with a cute little girl. I was up front and introduced myself, not knowing that they were there to meet one of our agent's and were his biggest clients.

"What's your name?" I asked the little girl.

"Cassie," she said, shaking my hand.

I asked the mom if I could show her something. I took her to our candy area and asked if she'd like to pick something. Her eyes widened and she exclaimed, "There's so much there!" I gave her a little bag and told her to pick out some of her favorites.

"That's not all!" I said, walking her to our ice cream freezer and opening the door. "Do you see something you like?"

"Can I have a Push-Up?" she asked, with a big smile. I then picked up one of the "Left, Right, Center" dice games that we put in our goodie bags. I asked her if she'd ever heard of it.

"No," she said. "I've never played that."

"Then, take it with you," I said. "You and your parents are going to have a blast!"

When we walked back out front, our agent was there getting ready to take them to look at a house. Cassie asked, "Tiffany, are you going to be here when we come back?"

I said, "I should be!"

She replied, "I'd really like to see you again."

They bought a house that day. Was it because their daughter got a bag of candy? Not necessarily, but one thing is certain. That happy moment put the whole family in a good mood and set them on a path to having a great day and a fantastic showing experience. Our encounter also set me up to have a good day.

A week later, I found an adorably hand-drawn card on my desk. It said: "Dear Tiffany, Thank you so much for all of the treats and snacks you gave me. The snacks were real tasty and the game was really fun. I really appreciate you. You are the best. Love, Cassie."

Was my moment with her about selling a house? Not at all. The moment was about delighting her, bringing a little bit of unexpected joy. Surprise and delight. That's an unforgettable incentive.

I've had the incredible opportunity to learn from Tony Robbins on multiple occasions. During a five-day Business Mastery program I attended at his private studio in West Palm Beach, my ears perked up when he said there are really only two basic functions for the business enterprise: marketing and innovation. **The goal of any successful business is to add more value than anyone else in your industry in a way that is unique to you, so people choose you over the competition — incentive!**

Tony explains that marketing is simply figuring out how to get someone to do business with you over and over again. The absolute key is that you must fall in love with your clients or customers and not your product or service. Think about that.

You bring more value to your clients when you realize you don't have a business without them, so you must love them and market to their needs. How do you do that? Find the incentive. Create what Tony calls an "irresistible offer," something that you offer in service or knowledge that no one else has. Then, overdeliver. Your ultimate goal is to become more valuable than others in your field.

Your service or product's "differentiating factor" is another incentive. What makes it unique? When Domino's Pizza expanded beyond the college campus market into residential delivery, they went up against many competitors. While visiting one of his stores, founder Tom Monahan happened to answer a call and heard a customer complaining about how long it took to get his pizza delivered. At that moment, Tom had his epiphany for the company's differentiating factor. The Domino's 30-minute delivery guarantee was born. That "get it quick" incentive became the driving force that catapulted Domino's to lots of dough! As Tony Robbins says, resources are never the problem. The problem is the lack of resourcefulness. Operate from opportunity, not limitation.

My incentive for selecting our office location was exactly that. I spotted an opportunity. I was drawn to an area a bit off the main drag — a charming mixed-used complex that housed retail, restaurants, and residential in multi-colored buildings on Naples Bay. Water is always an incentive for me. Throw in a little color, and it's a win. I fell in love with the spot and decided to secure an office there. Despite my excitement, I was overrun with naysayers who were quick to tell me, "It's suicide to open an office there. The big guys have already tried it and failed. What makes you think you will succeed?"

Those worrywarts didn't deter me in the least. They didn't know that

> "We're all equal as souls, but we're not equal in the marketplace. Your job is to become more valuable!"
>
> Tony Robbins

my shopping mall days taught me how to pull in traffic. Further, the developer was offering me incentives if I could bring more people to the area. Thus began an unforgettable journey, one that's allowed me to be resourceful, to create and promote events that we could brand to our company. Our events set the stage for the Bayfront to begin to boom. Commercial spaces started to fill, followed by an uptick in residential units. That leap was twelve years ago, and the rest is history.

"Things do not happen. Things are made to happen."

John F. Kennedy

If we opened our office where it was "normal" or sat behind our desks or went to trade shows and handed out pens, we would have had the barest minimum of engagement. Our events, from family concerts to the Stone Crab Festival, gave experiential incentives for people to flock to the streets in front of our office. Tony was right. It was opportunity. By adding value to the area, we created an audience and our business blossomed.

Over preparation can be another incentive you can give to make people want to work with you and buy what you're selling. This effort builds confidence, and confidence leads to trust.

A recent walk-through of a home we sold led to an interesting discussion with a very satisfied seller, an uber-successful businessman from Canada, who said he wanted to share something with me. "We looked at the other three open houses held in the neighborhood the day you held ours," he recounted. "We were wowed by the fact that our house had 20 or so cars parked outside, while the others had two or three. The difference was all the exciting things you did to announce it, and you made our house look welcoming, from the custom signs to the beautiful roses you had at the door." He said it was clear we had a strategy. "We knew that day we had picked the right sales team."

He wasn't just being nice. He was talking about business. While the couple was tending to important issues out of the country, we handled the transaction from soup to nuts. "From the get-go, you gave us enormous trust in you," he said. "We just want to thank you. You took the stress away and lightened our load."

Earned trust is a great incentive. Taking someone's stress away? That yields a raving fan. And what do raving fans do? They rave! In case no one's whispered it to you, word-of-mouth marketing is perhaps the most powerful form of advertising. Studies have shown that nine out of 10 consumers will trust a friend's recommendations over traditional media. Word-of-mouth marketing is the original social media phenomenon, and how do we get word-of-mouth promotion? By exceeding expectations, providing good customer service, and giving WOW at every opportunity.

Present people a reason to brag about what you did for them, and more customers will be knocking on your door.

 INQUIRY: What are you selling? Are you giving someone a reason to brag about it?

Early in my career, an amazing salesperson taught me about the "perception of value." Regardless of any market's state, there is always a value proposition that comes into play with any product or service. Your task is to listen to your customer's needs, assess how your product or situation fulfills those needs, and then convey the perception of value for what you're offering. This can be sharing a story on how the product is special, or the service will better their lives, or help them picture the desired outcome.

Sometimes it's as simple as sharing some background or history that surrounds a product. For example, if you're at a restaurant where Elvis frequented and always ordered the apple pie, the perception of value is that what's being served is "no normal slice of pie." It's an extraordinary, Elvis-loving slice of pie. Perception of value? High! The restaurant might charge a higher price for that slice or be the one to visit simply because Elvis ate there. In sharing a piece of factual history, they've created a unique selling proposition and an incentive to try it. The story elevates the value. If Elvis didn't eat it, "this is my grandma's recipe" also has a delightfully attractive sweetness.

There's no silver bullet on incentive. It is often a series of right choices, as well as your management of thought and energy. There's a positive reaction

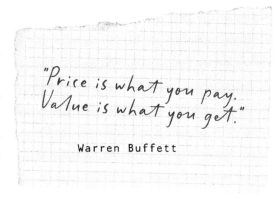

"Price is what you pay. Value is what you get."

Warren Buffett

to positive action. **If you want thoughtfulness, be thoughtful. If you want compliments, be complimentary. If you want to be heard, listen.**

The other day after a pitch, I was having lunch with one of our agents. We were feeling happy and positive about life and business. As we were leaving, a table of young women stopped us and one of them said, "We just want to tell you that you girls look very nice today."

I said, "Oh, thank you! That's super sweet."

"Really!" another added. "We've been talking about it and felt we had to tell you." As we walked to the car, my agent said, "It's so nice to have someone give you a compliment. I feel like in our day-to-day world we don't get them enough. As a matter of fact, I'm telling my husband all the time that he never flatters me. I could feel like a million bucks when we're going out somewhere, and he never seems to notice. It's been a source of contention for us. I'm like, 'Can't you just say that I look really nice tonight?'"

"Let me ask you something," I said. "Do you ever compliment him? Thank him for doing something extra or say that he looks hot? Do you ever reciprocate?"

"Oh my God," she said. "I never really thought about it that way."

"The Universe gives you back what you put out," I said.

If you're an entrepreneur, know this: the world is your audience. You want your audience to applaud. For them to do that, you need to give them a reason. Quite simply, people like to do business with someone they like, someone who makes them feel good. Think about what incentive you're offering. Your energy should be magnetic. Sitting on a stump and talking about the weather isn't going to do it.

As an example, my chiropractor's energy is always great. I look forward to seeing him, even though the "pops" scare me. While he's adjusting me, he always makes me laugh by telling me silly dad jokes. He stands out because he makes a bone-popping experience pleasurable. I leave his office aligned, but I also leave with my psyche a notch higher, happier, with extra bounce in my step. I will never go anywhere else because this man is just so delightful. He gives me the incentive to choose him over other options in town. For real, he cracks me up!

INQUIRY: Do you have any jokes in your bag of tricks? Something that can bring a laugh or a smile?

In my business life, my daily hope is to bring a little joy. It's as uncomplicated as that. Right before we went into the COVID lockdown, a lot of our clients were elderly, many of them were alone and, as we all were, they were frightened. We wanted to give them something that would put smiles on their faces. We used social media to announce that we wanted to drop a little gift off to our clients. All they had to do was direct message us their address. We teamed with local florists and created "Brighten Your Day" bouquets and Homebound Fun Boxes filled with games, treats, and activities like flowerpots with seeds for our clients with children.

The response was so great that we masked up and assisted the florists in delivering half of the bouquets. To keep everyone safe and prevent physical contact, we dropped gifts on people's doorsteps. It was a genuine moment of giving from our hearts. There was no business expectation, just a positive connection, a kind presence without being present. That was it. We delivered and sent out more than a hundred gifts, costing less than $2,000. We received many thanks and, after the COVID clouds lifted, business came as a result.

My personal incentive has never been money. I'm all about building solid relationships because I know good relationships mean good business and great business makes for great relationships. My ex-Lou used to always say, "I've never seen someone work so hard and not care about the money." But my mother's words continue to reign supreme. She always told me, **"If you work hard and do the right thing, the money will always come."**

During my years of struggle when money was not growing on the proverbial tree, I remember praying to God in a down moment, "I don't understand. My mom always said, "Do the work and rewards will follow." I got my answer when a friend shared a quote by Leo Buscaglia with me: "Your talent is God's gift to you. What you do with it is your gift back to God." Bam! It hit me.

My talent is elevating experiences for others, doing the extra things that make people feel good. Once I capitalized and underlined that, everything fell in line. From my encounter with my grocery bagger to providing market knowledge and great service to my sellers, my goal is to make even the smallest interactions positive ones. I want my actions to show others that I care. What I get in return are great connections and financial success.

If you're an entrepreneur and you're not authentically using your gifts to give everyone an incentive to work with you, you are negotiating at a disadvantage on the value of your product or service and missing out on the INth Degree power of incentive. Go all in and give people the reason that they HAVE to work with **YOU**.

Your sixth mission
INVEST IN YOURSELF

MISSION 6

Pharrell Williams literally incentivized the world to get happy with his smash hit "Happy." It garnered him a lot of fans. Put that on and give it a listen. Realize it's a gift to make others happy. It also creates long-lasting relationships. Now, turn the autopilot off and take some time to pay attention to what's going on around you. You can't solve a problem that you haven't noticed. Think about some things:

What's the first thing someone sees when they come into your business?

What's the greeting someone hears when they call your phone?

What extra thoughtfulness or "gift with purchase" do you give your customers and potential customers?

_____

_____

_____

_____

_____

When was the last time you sent a client a "thinking of you" gift or note?

_____

_____

_____

_____

If you want to grow your business, you must figure out what you're giving, not selling. Are you offering happiness? Joy? Wellness? Ease? Fun? The real gift of your product or service is what makes it (and you) valuable to your clients. **Give them that incentive and they will be happy and, in turn, return over and over!**

INFLUENCE

KEY 7

THE CAPACITY TO HAVE AN EFFECT ON THE CHARACTER, DEVELOPMENT, OR BEHAVIOR OF SOMEONE OR SOMETHING.

IT'S YOUR SUPERPOWER.

There's a lot of talk these days about "influencers," and there are plenty of people and things out there that are certainly trying to shape our thoughts and decisions. We are constantly inundated by people and information trying to persuade us, manipulate our behavior, and dance a little dance in our heads, from social media to the news, advertisements to the Nigerian man who keeps writing to me about the $6.5 million in Euros he wants to send me! Indeed, we've all seen the gorgeous people living their perfect lives with their big followings on TikTok and Instagram. We've heard them share how their weighted blanket is "just the thing" we need to sleep better or how their recommended face serum will magically iron all the wrinkles out.

But here's the thing: YOU are an influencer.

If you reach the last page of this book taking one thing to heart, it's that your life matters and how you go about your day matters to others.

From the moment you wake up each morning, you influence your-self, your family, even your dog. You influence the barista who makes your coffee. You influence the person sitting in the car next to you at the traffic light. You influence the first person you see at the office — and the last. You influence every single person you encounter, and because your actions create a ripple, your influence resonates and affects the lives of countless others. So, how do we make these moments, our moments, meaningful?

Think about it. That person at the coffee shop who said your hair looked good, added a little extra bounce in your step. The best bagger at the farmer's market who said she was glad to see you, warmed your heart. The nice man who let you cut in front of him in traffic when you were about to miss your turn, made your morning easier. These are actual things I experienced today while I've been out in the world. Prior to that, before I even left my house, the music I played while getting ready, the motivational YouTube video I watched, the quote from "The Secret" app I read, and Penny's cheery spunk, all influenced my day.

I was out recently for a mind-clearing walk along the bay in front of our office when two little girls, maybe four years old, were toddling along the waterfront with a babysitter. One had a balloon, and the other was blowing bubbles. They were happily singing John Denver's "Take Me Home, Country Roads."

"Country roads, take me home. To the place, I belong..." I joined in. "Mountain mama..." They giggled. I giggled. The babysitter giggled. It was a joyful moment that brought back the happy memory of a bedroom sing-along with my sister and cousin and our curling iron microphone. The little girls gave me a John Denver earworm, and I happily sang that song for the rest of the day. They influenced me. Two four-year-old, bubble-blowing girls made my day better.

Why wouldn't you want to be someone who makes the day better? If you want to be significant, to stand out, then be the person who brings joy and elevates someone else's experience.

"Since you get more joy out of giving joy to others, you should put a good deal of thought into the happiness that you are able to give."

Eleanor Roosevelt

> *"Find a place inside where there's joy, and the joy will burn out the pain."*
>
> Joseph Campbell

You'll find it also elevates yours.

My childhood pain doesn't cross my mind often, but when it does, it's a visceral jolt, a flash of ten-year-old Tiff walking into a funeral home full of people, with all their eyes staring at my mom, sister, and me. What does a ten-year-old know about funerals and the sorrow it represents? I recall scanning the room, looking for encouragement, and only seeing concern in the gaze of the onlookers. I remember hoping it wasn't real, that my dad was alive, and that this was all a bad dream.

As we approached the open casket, I peered inside. There he lay, not looking at all like himself, but recognizable, nonetheless. I can remember staring at him and waiting for his eyes to open. They didn't. The rest of the funeral remains a blur of thoughts, tears, and an unyielding pit in my stomach.

When we got home, my mom's typical good nature was noticeably absent. She was not herself, and our house had a cloud of sadness hanging over it. It was Christmas break from school, but our festive mood was gone. Our holiday joy had been sent to heaven, or at least my little Catholic heart hoped it so.

After my dad's death and the resulting despair, I realized how important it was that we didn't continue to feel like that. I didn't want to dwell in the torment of what we could have done differently or how we might have changed the outcome, and I certainly didn't want to see my mom agonizing in unhappiness either. I made a conscious decision to make the sadness go away.

It was 1980, and therapy wasn't a typical thing, certainly not readily accessible in small town Ohio. Although I am quite confident some type of counseling could have helped me deal with my feelings, I had to climb out of the sorrow myself. Fortunately, I had some great influences to help me do that.

Shortly after my father passed away, an agreement was made between my mom and Grandma Frank, my dad's mother, and Aunt

Bev, my dad's sister. On the third weekend of every month, from then until I graduated high school, my sister and I would head over for a sleepover, alternating between their houses, which were conveniently located across from each other. My sister Monica and I were always excited to be dropped off, barely saying goodbye to our mom as we ran off to start our stay.

From pushing each other to unreasonably high heights on my cousin's tree swing to walking to the corner store with a dollar to get a slushy, those weekends were a pure delight. On Grandma Frank's weekends, she'd make us our favorite creamy scrambled eggs, which we deemed the best eggs in the history of breakfast. She'd accompany that with her perfectly toasted bread from her circa 1950s toaster with the cloth cord, which she'd cover edge to edge in a scoop of her homemade black currant jelly. (What I wouldn't give for that toast and jelly, right now!) But the real culinary specialty was her orange Jell-O, which was always hiding some kind of fruit or vegetable, from carrots to cabbage to marshmallows.

Aunt Bev's house was a whole other experience. She'd always let us pick a favorite spot to eat out, from the local pizzeria to a little hamburger joint that had horse saddles for bar stools. My Aunt is forever in my heart as "The Queen of Delighting." She always found a way to do special things not only for us, but for others. Known affectionately by everyone as "Aunt Bev," she has always gone the extra mile with her thoughtfulness and warm feelings to bring joy to everything from special holidays to day-to-day moments. Aunt Bev is an influencer. Gifts aside, her presence is always a present.

Those weekends with my dad's family were influential in teaching me about making others feel seen, heard, and unconditionally loved. We didn't go to see them out of obligation. We went because of how we felt when we were there. They made us feel joyful.

Now that I'm running a business, I realize that's exactly how you want your team and your clients to feel. Happy! You want them to want to see you. **My simple goal every day is to use my influence to lift others up, to bring joy. It doesn't just make for good business. It makes for a good life.**

The reality is that we all have (and will continue to have) occasional rain on our parades. My dad's death (and its aftermath) was a tremendous turning point in my life and is certainly part of my story. Like the other life events that may have sunk me, from my harsh breakup to business struggles, I made the choice to swim, influencing myself to act. Instead of letting these unpleasant things swallow my hope, I accept hardships to be part of my journey, hurdles if you will, that spur me to find ways over, under, or around to remain happy and grateful and to bring happiness, to do good things, to shine.

Recently, I was driving home after an afternoon riddled with emotion at the office. What started as an incredible day full of great news and fun activity, turned into a surplus of challenges, rotten issues served up one after another. It was as if the Universe did a complete about-face on me, like Florida weather in the summer, a bright, beautiful morning followed by dark skies and afternoon storms.

I had heaviness in both my head and heart. Each blow of my day was jockeying for position to lead the parade. During my drive home, I made a decision to stop the parade and said out loud to myself, "Tiff, you are not going to let anyone or anything steal your joy today!" With that, I turned my attention to gratitude for both the incredible things and those that were hard to believe. I thanked the Universe for its plan, for the blessings I've been given, for the nice, air-conditioned car I was driving, for the ability to pick my favorite song with a click of a button. I put on Katy Perry and drove on. I expressed gratitude for the gorgeous trees and grass that are bright green this time of year, for the ability to call this special community home and, as I pulled into my driveway, I said thanks for my house, my sanctuary and safe space, and the delight of knowing my little Penny's face was waiting to greet me behind the door.

"There are those who give with joy, and that joy is their reward."
Khalil Gibran

In my 25-minute drive home, I had gone from angst to warmth. It wasn't anything anyone else said or did. It was all me. I shed my worries, by reigniting my sense of gratitude. The power came from withIN. *I influenced myself.*

What happened next felt magical. I ran in, scooped Penny up, and we went out to her favorite park. We had a wonderful hour together, truly joyful. Had I not made the effort to turn my frown upside down, I would have missed out on a most excellent memory. Recognizing the good, influenced me to get over the bad.

We got home exhausted, but happy. Penny has this fluffy little donut bed on the floor by the sofa that has raised edges. Although I'm not certain when this little exercise began, it's a daily occurrence now. All I have to say to her is, "Do you want me to tuck you in?" She runs from wherever she is in the house and dive bombs into the middle of the donut. I go over and tuck her little body into the soft cushion, and she lays there, sweetly still in her satisfied splendor. It's the craziest, silliest thing, but every time she dives into her bed and looks up at me waiting for my tuck, my heart swells. She derives a great thrill from the moment, and the joy it brings me in seeing her light up, is the absolute best. **Sometimes it's the smallest things that can have the greatest influence.** I'm sure you have something that comes to mind, too.

INQUIRY: What are five things that bring you joy?

1. _____

2. _____

3. _____

4. _____

5. _____

Rest in these five and let this list influence your mood whenever you need it.

In the journal my mom wrote for me before she left the Earth, she said, "All those that know you and are loved by you, are truly blessed." This has become my marching orders. I share this with you, not in reference to myself, but in reference to YOU.

Your life and your uniqueness are a contribution you must make to the world. Don't get older. Get better. Take responsibility for the time you're here, for the spot you're given on this blue marble. Make the most of what you have been given and what you have to give. Though she's no longer with me, my mom's gifts continue to influence my life. Her advice lives on, I hear her voice often, as do her delicious recipes, which I love to make and share with others. (In the INformation Guide in the back of the book, I've given you some of my favorites from her collection including her Swedish meatballs, lemon cake, and chocolate chip cookies, Bruce's new obsession.)

This is the time to ask... What are you leaving behind? Not when you die, but in your wake, every moment you're alive. Let it be that someone remembers you because you were kind. Help others even when they can't help you back. Look for the good in everyone and point it out. Be the authentic, considerate, influential self you are, and your life will manifest greatness. **To make a difference in this world (and in your own business and life), you don't have to be brilliant, rich, or have a million followers, you just have to care.** It's the one time that it's good for you to have all the cares in the world!

Insight on INFLUENCE

Life is fragile, precious, and not to be taken for granted. I'm looking to squeeze the good out of every day and be grateful for it in all its wonder. My challenge to you is what if every day you get up and think to yourself, *Today I'm going to use my influence to plant as many little seeds of happiness that I can.* By giving joy, you'll find joy. Studies show that joyful people have better immune systems, lower stress, and longer lives. They also have reduced risk of a heart attack, lower cholesterol levels, and maintain a healthier blood pressure.

When I opened my own company, Barbara Corcoran, one of my biggest influencers, gave me an unforgettable piece of guidance. She said, "Tiffany, the joy truly is in the getting there." She's right. Sometimes we are focused so hard on climbing the mountain, we forget to take in the view. I'm here right now to give you some binoculars. **Look for the joy.**

Several years into my business, it became abundantly clear that I couldn't continue on the same mental path. I had gained so much strength from my journey, but I was struggling. I was losing steam. I spent so much time planning, worrying, and preparing for the future, that I forgot about the very important present. My team (to the point of exhaustion) has heard me say that the aim of great marketing or branding is to maintain a presence even when you're not present. Sounds great, right? Until I realized that I was not actually present. I was showing up physically, but mentally I was off trying to get us to that enchanted vision of where I wanted us to be, rather than being in the now. I felt I was going it alone, that all the weight of everyone's happiness was on my shoulders.

What turned it around? An outside perspective. In my adult life, after discovering my ex's affair, I found a professional to talk through life's issues. Dianne helped me deal with the crushing heartbreak and feelings of abandonment, which rekindled emotions from when my dad died. When I first met Dianne, she asked what I wanted to get out of our work together. I immediately said, "Please help me not become hard or bitter, but to maintain some naivety in my head and heart so I have the ability to always find the goodness."

Talk about influence. Dianne has become my biggest cheerleader and helped steer me through some of life's most rocky moments. Dianne's given great advice. For example, soon after my horrible breakup, she advised me to invest in all new sheets and bed linens. I got beautiful, girly ones that made me happy. It helped. When a vicious cycle of overthinking everything and self-doubt fueled sleepless nights and poor decisions, Dianne helped me correct course by advising me to find a place of peace where I could find calm.

The first place I thought of was an empty church. So, off I went to sit in a quiet church and just listen. The soft silence soothed my wild thoughts and gave me an awakening. I sat on that pew and realized that as a leader, I have to be my own influencer. Yes, I have an amazing team, but their interests, risks, and investments in the business aren't the same as mine. Leaders can't expect the same support they give. It's not a reciprocal arrangement, and ultimately, it requires the need for self-motivation, self-love, and self-encouragement.

I realized my job was to focus on today, knowing I had everything I needed within me to grow my business and face the challenges. I simply had to surrender to that and trust the outcome. What could I handle and do now? It was a pivotal life moment. There wasn't any hesitation. I made a formal agreement with myself that became set in stone. I was determined to build my business with kindness and do things from the heart out, rather than

"Paradise is where I am."

Voltaire

143

building the business and then trying to inject heart into it.

Think back to when you were a kid. All you wanted to do was play, and while we were playing, we were figuring out what we were going to do next to play some more. Organically, we were all about finding the joy. Candy brought us joy. Being outside brought us joy. Playing games with friends brought us joy. We could find happiness in simple things — riding a bike, drinking from the hose on a hot day, and playing kickball and flashlight tag in the yard.

When I was a kid, I found joy in making my mom happy. When she'd get home, I would have the dishes done, house organized, laundry washed, folded, and put away. I took great pride in seeing her smile and giving her a moment to exhale. I quickly realized witnessing these moments of delight in her face and her happy disposition did something to my insides. It made me feel joyful. As an added benefit, my joyful pursuits literally paid off. I became so good at accomplishing the tasks and found such happiness in it, my sister would pay me to clean her room!

It's only as we age, when life's struggles start to hit us, that our joy gets lost in the workaday shuffle.

As I've mentioned, for 16 years of my life, I loved to tap dance. It was my passion and a huge part of my becoming, but somehow, life got in the way. As with all of us, we did things we thoroughly enjoyed as a child, hobbies that brought us great pleasure, and they got lost in the adult shuffle. What happened to them? And why?

In a recent discussion with my team, I posed the question and listened as they wistfully shared happy things they did when they were young. Some loved to sew or crochet. Some said they enjoyed the simple act of sitting on a porch swing and having a talk with someone they cared about without any interruption from today's technology. Several spoke of sports they played, reading great books, going to concerts, making mix tapes, scrapbooking, taking long bike rides to nowhere, or just putting a pole in the water for a day of fishing. How can we bring that back into our lives? How can we influence ourselves to find that joy again in our high-pressure adult lives?

Now, as we open that last door, let me persuade you to find what happened to those joys of youth. My co-author Bruce recently pushed me (the influencer that he is!) to dust off my old tap shoes and try a little ditty. Surprisingly, the shoes didn't disintegrate, and even more surprising, my feet remembered the happy steps. I would like to think that dancing is just like riding a bike, but my body disagreed, and I had to work through some stiffness. Even still, I captured it on video and uploaded it to social media. That made me feel vulnerable, but since that first post, I can't stop thinking about it! Reconnecting with some childhood dance friends was a bonus. More and more often, I am finding my toes tapping under my desk, rethinking routines of yesteryear, and wondering what I should tackle next. That bit of encouragement gave me a burst of nostalgia and a renewed dose of delight that I didn't expect. It took me back to the joy of my youth, so freeing and refreshing.

The idea of it reminded me of the outfits my mom sewed for my dance competitions and how she'd sit in the audience to encourage me, to cheer me on. My tap shoes made me realize that I want to do more things that bring me delight and to spend more time helping give others those same feelings. I've started doing what I'm calling "Delight Days" where I find opportunities to bring totally unexpected bursts of happiness to someone (or a group of someones). As I was finishing this chapter, I took my entire team to the premiere of the Barbie® movie! These are the things that lift me up. Giving from the goodness of my heart, even in the days I wasn't sure how I was going to meet payroll or put gas in my car, has always opened the floodgates to allow me to receive.

Recently, I had clients who were moving overseas with their two children and, in advance of the closing, had already shipped all their personal items. I surprised them with a full-course dinner from a local

Italian restaurant and a nice bottle of wine. For the children, I put together a fun "party package" from Chuck E. Cheese with all the bells and whistles. I left the feast on their front doorstep and texted them to say it was there. What I didn't anticipate was their response, which brought me to tears. They said the whole family was smiling and thanked me for giving them a moment to exhale and creating one last wonderful memory in their home. It truly elevated my own night. Their joy had influenced my own. I went to bed remembering my mom's words that **"There is no characteristic more important in life than a good and giving heart."**

Positively influencing someone's day is the key to opening the "lack of" mindset that we sometimes get stuck in on life's journey. I've found that lack is a result of fear. Fear of not having enough, not doing enough, or being enough. In that fear, you are closed off and holding tight, super tight, with all you have just to get through. Abundance cannot flow when you are closed. It is only when we release our grip that goodness can flow out and come in.

Today, I choose to look for ways to influence a joyful mindset, especially when I'm feeling helpless. Elevating instead of escalating. Being courageous to make an impact — making someone happy or moving others closer to their goals — brings us closer to our own. It is a value-add for both business and life.

In her biography of Warren Buffett, *The Snowball: Warren Buffett and the Business of Life*, author Alice Schroeder tells the story of a question Buffett was asked by students when he gave a speech at the University of Georgia. They wanted to know his definition of success.

He said that as you approach the end of your life, your only real measure of success should be the number of "people you want to have love you actually do love you." He went on to say you could have hospital wings named for you but, "If you get to my age in life and nobody thinks well of you, I don't care how big your bank account is, your life is a disaster."

Look, we all make mistakes, but pencils have erasers for those who are willing to make corrections. To bring grace and love to the world, you first must find it for yourself. Not every day is perfect, but we should strive every day to be our best selves. So, ask yourself, who is that? That's not someone who complains about everything or lives with a victim mentality. That's someone who learns the lesson, takes accountability, and has a mindset of abundance. That's someone who is grateful and is looking to find and attract joy.

In my mind, it's one big circle. If I'm not feeling joy, I know I'm not feeling grateful. So, I quickly re-focus my attention on making a "things I'm thankful for" list. What happens (every time) is that this action reignites my joy. I can spring out my door, ready to go. Gratitude brings joy. Joy brings enthusiasm. That's the circle.

On one of my walks around Ava Maria, I came upon a pile of little sticks, perfectly formed and all about the same length. They seemed special to me, so I scooped them up. When I got in my car, I turned on a talk by Abraham. What did she say? She started talking about sticks! She explained that in life, there are two ends to every stick. One side is what you want, the other side is the absence of what is wanted. When I got back to the office, I immediately put my sticks in a cup on my desk as a daily reminder of that.

At my next Monday morning team meeting, we discussed getting from one end of the stick to the other. Let's say there's one of your listings that is not selling. You're frustrated. You think that everything you're doing is wrong. You're at the bad end of the stick, stuck, with absence of what is wanted. The only way to shift to the opposite end is to walk your way there with baby steps.

Negative space is "I can't move the property." Move toward the other end of the stick...

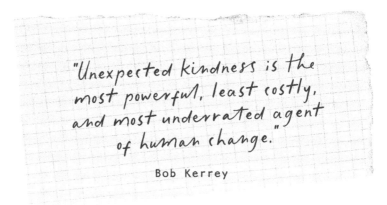

"Unexpected kindness is the most powerful, least costly, and most underrated agent of human change."

Bob Kerrey

The good thing is I have a listing. An active listing! Some people don't have a single listing.

The seller entrusted me to be their representation. They still believe in me.

I have showings. I know I'm the best person for the job.

I've been selling for 10 years. This will be another property to add to my "sold" list.

My skillset is showing a property's best features.

I'm going to give it some extra effort.

I'm making a few calls to other brokers who might have clients.

I'm sending emails to past clients who might know someone right for this property.

I'm calling the people who've already seen the house to see if they might want to come back for a second look.

I'm going to sell this house!

Most people don't understand that YOU are the influence who can take you from one end of the stick to another. You choose your side of the stick the moment you wake up. Once you say, "I'm in a bad mood," you've defined it. You've given it a label and you can't get to the other end without manifesting it otherwise.

As I was finishing this chapter and trying to influence you to find joy, The Secret app gave me some reinforcement. The post this morning suggested that taking a few minutes each day to be in joy and send love out to the world helps bring about greatness in your life. "The law of attraction matches the frequencies you send out and will return the love to you multiplied. When applied deeply and correctly, this exercise can completely change your life, and at the same time touch the lives of many."

INQUIRY: Think of someone who makes you smile the minute you see them. What role do they play in your life? How can you take their example and make others feel that very way?

We've been through a lot together, you and me. I hope I've influenced you to go All IN to look for positive ways you can stand out. I encourage you to take the keys from this book and unlock a lot of doors.

Don't give up or succumb to the naysayers or to life's occasional blows. Be **INTREPID**.

Get up each morning with eagerness and be **INVIGORATED**.

Find your purpose and know your **INTENTION**.

Look for people and things that **INSPIRE** you.

Use your creativity to discover ways to be innovative and original. Open your mind with **INGENUITY**.

Understand what makes people want to work with you. Give them that **INCENTIVE**.

And, finally, realize that the master key to all of this is your **INFLUENCE**. What kind of effect do you want to have? What kind of influence do you want to be? And how are you going to use that power?

This is a good day. I encourage you to do things you enjoy, be grateful for what you have, make your ultimate desire to empower others, and have a positive impact on the world.

The one thing I can assure you if you really want to stand out and be remembered is this: leave people feeling better about themselves. **Bring *your* joy to the world!**

Your seventh mission
INVEST IN YOURSELF

MISSION 7

In honor of my four-year-old, bubble blowing influencers, give a listen to "Take Me Home, Country Roads" by John Denver. The heartfelt lyrics resonate with joy, which is why it's been covered by more than 150 artists in at least 19 languages!

Next up, listen to "Joy" by Andy Grammer. It's energizing and empowering. Grammer said this about the song: "I have always loved the word 'Joy.' I feel like it has a depth, a grounded spiritual center, something deeper and more substantial than happiness. It's somehow light and weighty at the same time. I wanted to capture all that while still having a party."

And, finally, to round out our joyful influence and our final *INth Degree* track, let's play "Joy to the World" by Three Dog Night loud and proud. The last event I did before moving to Florida was overseeing the Vocal Group Hall of Fame induction ceremony in Sharon, Pennsylvania. A massive celebratory concert followed the event with Chuck Negron of Three Dog Night the last to perform. I asked him to perform his favorite song. What did he sing? "Joy to the World." There wasn't a dry eye in the crowd. Play it and be IN joy with it.

Since social media is one of the most all-encompassing influencers of modern times, our final mission is to approach social media differently. Years ago, I made a commitment to regularly post on social media to create a presence for my business. That's grown into a daily opportunity. I hold myself accountable to post something heartwarming or motivational before 8 a.m. That helps set the tone for my day. This year, I made a New Year's resolution to respond to posts with a heart, rather than the simple thumbs up and to only respond to posts that I could "heart" genuinely. It's created a different experience, one that is more thoughtful in my reaction and that creates more retention from that action. This leaves me with a smile and a happier heart.

Let's start with this: what are your three favorite quotes? (If you don't have favorites, try Googling "quotes about" and a word that gives you a charge like "life" or "motivation" or "vacation." Or grab any of the great quotes from this book.)

Write them here:

1. _____

2. _____

3. _____

Now, what are three things that bring you joy? It could be a love, flowers, pizza, dogs... whatever makes you joyful.

Write them here:

1. _____

2. _____

3. _____

For the next week, turn your social media into these joyful things. The quotes, the things that bring you joy, and photos that bring you a smile. Influence your followers with this goodness and then delight in the feedback. As you go through the week, make a point to scroll through others' offerings with the goal of finding things that make you feel good. When you spot them, give those posts a heart or a positive comment wishing people joy in their day. In doing so, you're standing out by inviting people into goodness. This small step in how you choose to approach your social media will flip the switch on the negative of such platforms into a positive game changer for your mental powers.

Let's take that action item and amplify it by making your purpose for one week to bring some joy to the world in a way that feels right for you — big or small — and see how it makes you feel. **One thing is certain, when you're IN joy, it will make you stand out! Joy is a giant welcome mat that invites people IN.**

Tiffany McQuaid
INFORMATION GUIDE

While working on this book, I discovered a lot of interesting and fun things that you might like to try or explore. There are some inspirational, motivational, and life-expanding podcasts like Guy Raz's _"How I Built This,"_ and Barbara Corcoran's _"Business Unusual."_ I have the best YouTube videos from Oprah Winfrey, Tony Robbins, Brene Brown, and Abraham Hicks. And I also have a few other surprises!

SCAN QR CODE FOR ONLINE LINKS
TO THINGS THAT WILL INSPIRE YOU!

Mom's delicious recipes
IN THE KITCHEN

Here's something special. Since I told you how much my mom always loved a "gift with purchase" (ALL of us do!) here you'll find some of her favorite recipes, including:

Barbeque Chip Chop, which was a staple at all family gatherings, likely because it was economical, but loved by all!

The Lemon Cake, which was everyone's favorite and still is to this day. I promise the lemony glaze will delight you when you take your first bite.

Mom's pickles, which have always been a family favorite. These are easy to make and the best on a sandwich top or to pop one into your mouth!

The Prize Cake, which always created raving fans…

From my house to yours. Enjoy!

♡ Tiffany

STRAWBERRY GLAZE PIE

1 qt fresh strawberries
1 cup sugar
¼ tsp salt
1½ cups water
3 tbsp cornstarch

2 tbsp lemon juice
1/8 tsp red food coloring
One baked cooled
9 inch pie shell

Hull berries, wash. Measure one cup; reserve rest. Mash the 1 cup berries, add sugar, salt and one cup of water. Heat to boiling. Blend cornstarch with remaining water; add to berry mixture. Cook, stirring constantly, until clear. Add lemon juice; combine with remaining cup of who berries. Pour into pie shell; refrigerate until serving time

Belinda's Frozen pickles

2 qts cucumbers--sliced not too thin
2 medium onions sliced thin
1 T salt

Mixwell and let stand 2 hours.

Solution: 2 cups white vinegar and 2
                cups sugar.

Heat this--do not boil--cool completely
Pour over cucumbers-mix well and pack
in freezer containers.

PRIZE CHOCOLATE CAKE

Cream 2/3 cup shortening with 2 cups sugar
Add 2 eggs and beat well

Sift together 2 cups flour
              $\frac{1}{2}$ cup cocoa
              $\frac{1}{2}$ t salt
Add alternately to creamed mixture with 1 cup
thick sour milk-buttermilk. Add1 t vanilla
Blend 2 t soda with 1 cup boiling water
Add to cake mixture. Bake 350 degrees
25 to 30 minutes
                              Over

ICING

$\frac{1}{4}$ lb marg.
$1\frac{1}{2}$ cup conf sugar   - chocolate
1 egg

CHOCOLATE CHIP COOKIES

1 cup butter or margarine, soft
1 cup firmly packed brown sugar
1 cup granulated sugar
2 eggs
1 tsp vanilla
2 cups sifted all-purpose flour
1 tsp soda
3/4 tsp salt
3 cups rolled oats uncooked
1 cup (6oz.) pkg semi-sweet chocolate pieces
½ cup chopped walnuts   over

Heat oven to 375. Beat butter and sugars together until creamy; blend in eggs and vanilla. Sift together flour, soda, salt. Add to creamed mixture, beating well. Stir in oats, chocolate pieces and walnuts. Drop by teaspoonfuls unto ungreased cookie sheets. Bake 10 to 12 minutes.--Yields 6 dozen

---

Swedish Meatballs

3 slices bread, crumbled
1/3 cup milk
1=1b ground beef
1 small onion grated
½ t salt
¼ t peper
Dash ground nutmeg
2 T cooking oil
1 packet brown gravy mix
½ cup mayonnaise

Add bread to milk. Mix in next 5 ingredients. Shape into 1 inch balls. Chill. Brown meatballs in oil in large skillet. Prepare gravy according to directions using 1¼ cups water. Blend in Mayonnaise. Add to meat balls and heat. Makes about 45 meatballs.

Scalloped Cabbage

½ medium size head of cabbage
½ cup cracker crumbs
1½ cups milk
2 tbsp butter — 1 tsp salt

Grease casserole. Shred cabbage. Alternate layers cabbage & crumbs. Salt each cabbage layer. Warm milk — 1 tbsp butter. Pour over cabbage. Dot 1 tbsp butter. Sprinkle with paprika. Bake 1 hr — 350°

LEMON CAKE

1 pkg cake mix--white or yellow
1 pkg lemon jello
3/4 cup oil
3/4 cup water
4 eggs.   Bake 350 - 30 minutes in 9x13
                  pan.

As soon as cake comes out of oven punch
hole in top with toothpic. Spoon over
icing made with 2 cups conf sugar, rind
and juice of 2 lemons.

CHIP CHOP HAM FOR HOT SANDWICHES

1¼ lbs chopped ham
1 small bottle catsup
1 small onion grated or chopped
1 tsp celery seed
1 chopped green pepper
1 Tbsp worchestershire sauce
1 Tbsp sugar

Mix all sauce ingredients & cook about
20 minutes before adding chopped ham.
Put on buns and wrap in foil
Heat in oven 275 degrees - 20 minutes

Tiffany McQuaid
INTH DEGREE PLAYLIST

Want to get happy? Well then, listen up! A 2013 study published in *The Journal of Psychology* found that when people listen to upbeat music, they are more successful at thinking happy thoughts. Ask any teenager and they'll tell you that music boosts our mood, but new research is showing it's actually great for your mental health. The Global Council on Brain Health has found music has a beneficial effect on dopamine, the brain's pleasure chemical and boosts oxytocin, the "love hormone."

So, with all that in mind... let's crank up our *INth Degree* playlist. Our house DJ will continually add new songs to keep the beat going! **Access the playlist with this QR code.**

"Unstoppable"	Sia
"Me Too"	Meghan Trainor
"I Feel Good"	Pitbull
"Good to Be Alive"	Andy Grammer
"Rise Up"	Andra Day
"Firework"	Katy Perry
"Simply the Best"	Tina Turner
"Over the Rainbow/ Wonderful World"	Robin Schulz, Alle Farben, and Israel Kamakawiwo'ole
"Happy"	Pharrell Williams
"Take Me Home, Country Roads"	John Denver
"Joy"	Andy Grammer
"Joy to the World"	Three Dog Night
"Roar"	Katy Perry

IN ACKNOWLEDGEMENT

With each step along this journey there have been many who have come and gone, but these are the ones that have made the most impact and left the biggest stamp on my head and heart:

To my sister, Monica Jones, who has endured the ride alongside me. Through all our ups and downs, twists and turns, she has shown tremendous strength and has become a leader in life and business, and I couldn't be prouder of the woman she has become. Mom and Dad would be too...

Although most of our family has since left the earth, each member has left a special mark or memory on my life that I will never forget. Aunt Bev, the "Queen of Delighting," who has always made my heart smile, and for that I will be eternally grateful. My "creative" cousin Melody Waicukewith who adds a little extra flair to everything she does. My most handsome nephew Alex Jones, who I adore and am confident has inherited the entrepreneurial gene. Lastly, to my Grandma Frank, who has passed, but her special gifts and ingenuity will forever live on.

An extra special thanks to Dianne Durante. Her guidance has protected my head and heart and kept me from becoming hard and negative. She has extended nothing short of an unwavering and incredible belief in me and my capabilities at a time or times when I may not have believed in myself, and that has made a permanent mark on my soul.

I would like to share a special amount of gratitude and love to Helen Constantine who has given me unwavering support. She started with me on my real estate journey when I was fresh into the business, and despite her retirement several years ago, has been a right arm for me and has never left my life, nor Penny's...

To the incredible Molly McKinley, thank you so much for hearing me and seeing me. But more importantly, believing in me. Without that, none of this would have been possible. Thank you for being so thoughtful and insightful, you are appreciated more than you know, as is your team at Redtail Creative. Beth Brant you are incredibly gifted, and I have been honored to work with you. Wendy Gatlin and Shelly Leslie thank you for sharing your special knowledge. You are all a collective group of talented individuals.

"The journey of a thousand miles begins with a single step."

Lao Tzu

I have been blessed with a handful of incredible mentors in my life, but the one that has had the most impact is Barbara Corcoran. When I first encountered this amazing person two decades ago, women leaders in real estate were not common, she gave me aspiration, determination, and a swift kick in the pants when I needed it. Thank YOU, Barbara, for taking me under your wing. You have made such a huge difference in my life, left your thumbprint on my business, and will always hold an incredibly special part of my heart.

My world has been touched by some super special friends who have been a part of me from the early years and have stuck close, and some newer friends that have an incredibly special place in my heart, you know who you are...

There have been so many mentors who have touched me and are a part of this book, whether they know it or not. That is the beauty of our world today, we all have access to people and insight when we need it, whether in person or from a portal, it is a choice to seek it, but one that can impact our lives greatly. From Pat Lewis to Amy Noll, Jim Winner and Ann Levitan, thank you for your guidance and inspiration throughout my various stages. With deep thanks to Katy Perry whose creativity has inspired me to let mine authentically shine. To Esther Hicks & Abraham, your gifts shared have been a huge part of my ability to overcome and to be open to life in a way I never thought possible. To Tony Robbins, who seemingly selflessly pushes messages of hope and shares knowledge that has the power to change worlds, if you are willing to listen. To Gabby Bernstein, Wayne Dyer, Louise

Hay, Oprah, Lady Gaga, Jay Shetty, Dolly Parton and the list goes on, all of you have shared messages that have resonated with me in one way or another. May you continue to inspire others the way you have me.

This dream come true would never have happened without the incredible Bruce Littlefield, who has so beautifully crafted this message with his special flair. Through the incredible power of the Universe, after a few seeds were planted, this project was born and has grown into something beyond anything that I could have dreamt of. Our intent is that this shared collaboration conveys a message of HOPE. Bruce, thank YOU for all of this. You are a gifted addition to my life and to this world. Also, to Scott Stewart, I so appreciate your support of this venture, of Bruce, and for your incredible chocolate chip cookie making skills!

To my neighbors in Quail Creek Estates, thank you for sharing your homes and community with me for the last 21 years. My heart lives here for sure. For our "office neighbors" at Bayfront, we are so thankful to be in your backyard for the last 12 years in a variety of capacities. A special thank you to Kevin Stoneburner for your belief in us over all this time. I would be remiss not to mention Naples, this town that we LOVE and are proud to call our HOME base.

Last, but certainly not least, to my chosen family... every single one of them, at McQuaid & Company. Boy, have we been through a lot together over the last decade, but you are each the reason why I persist. It's not often in business that you find yourself surrounded by a group of people that you feel blessed to work with every day. Despite the obstacles, there is true caring and passion at the core of what we do and who we are. That is our uniquely us "special sauce" and for that dynamic, I am grateful.

So, to the "core" of who we are: Adam Brown, our collective creativity and your special talents have been the vision that turned something from nothing. A truly amazing feat! Nicholas Jankowski, I always saw your tremendous gifts, even from your very young age. It has been a pleasure to build this with you and watch you evolve into the incredible leader you are. Nicole Hogue, from when we first met, you were a gift. Your skills and maternal touches are an integral part of our growth, and I cannot wait to see what you can lead us into next. Krista Fogelsong, you are so very talented, and I am thankful to be innovating with you, the true sweetheart of Southwest Florida. Eric Loya, your special abilities, enthusiasm, creativity, and willingness to always step in anywhere needed, is quite simply a delight and so appreciated. Bottom line is YOU, "the core" are ALL loved beyond measure, and I am honored to work with you as we weave our talents and gifts together to make TRUE real estate and business magic.

To our McFamily of Realtors, from the OG's Scott Leiti, Gail DeFrancesca and Rob Mauceli, who have stuck by us since the very beginning, to those that have been on and joined our journey at varying capacities including: Tony Grech, Roy Head, Nancy Burgess, David Gross, Sarah Chelnik, Lynn Koch, Anthony Montella, Sandra Banks, Karla Werchek, Naila Torrens, Jean Dery, Sue Foy, Rick Dery, Sue Santolli, Rosalinda Lopez, Ana Alonso, Julia Wolfswinkel, Dale Kubala, Karen Ball, Miriam Lemoine, Susan Birchenough, Adam Martin, Bernard Cordero, Heather Winter, Anthony Seling, John Dugan, Shawn Strodeski, Amy Tencza, Stephen Kalman, Shelby Barrett, Marianne Lebesky, Natalie Fox, Sylvia Bocwinski, Matt Steves, Beth Montoya and all the other incredible people, including Attorney Ian Holmes, Attorney Danielle Simmons, Ana Alonso, Michael Perel, Ryan Serhant, Michael Whalen, and Jerry Maxson, who we have the immense pleasure of working with now and in the future.

Finally, I would like to express my love and total gratitude to my mom, Belinda, who showed me every day that strength is learned, grace is an application, and that you have a choice every day to decide how you want to show up for life. She was a force and her love for us was the true blessing. To my dad, David, who was a light despite his inner demons, and always brought a smile to the faces of everyone he encountered. Through his weakness, I learned strength. But more importantly, I learned from him that no matter what, never forget to hang in, because tomorrow is a new day and there is ALWAYS HOPE. For that I am eternally grateful....

—♡ Jeffang

Tiffany McQuaid
INTH DEGREE SHOP

Let's go ShopIN' where inspiration meets imagination in the most delightful way.

Dive IN to our online store where you'll find a treasure trove of our favorite things that will take your life to "The INth Degree."

Access the Shop with this QR code.

AUTHOR BIOS

TIFFANY MCQUAID is an innovator nationally recognized for building an independent real estate brokerage that holds big agency power. As President of McQuaid & Company Real Estate Services, she has made quite an impact on the real estate industry. Her office, located in Naples, Florida, specializes in residential real estate and new construction and development representation all over Southwest Florida. She speaks regularly on national platforms sharing her unique marketing strategies and building a business with caring at its core. She is Mom to her little long-haired Dachshund, Penny. You can find Tiffany at her office in the heart of Downtown Naples, or globally at **TiffanyMcQuaid.com.**

For more motivation and inspiration, follow **@tiffanymcquaidcom.**

BRUCE LITTLEFIELD is a best-selling author, lifestyle expert, and arbiter of American culture. Hailed as a "lifestyle authority" by *The New York Times* and as a "modern-day Erma Bombeck" by NPR, he is a contributor to Good Morning America and has appeared on NBC's Today show, CBS's Early Show and ABC's The View, as well as MSNBC, Rachael Ray, The Soup, and The Better Show. He has authored nineteen books, including *Garage Sale America*, *Merry Christmas, America!*, and *Airstream Living*, all critically acclaimed adventures in Americana. His *Bedtime Book for Dogs* is the first book written with words dogs understand and kids love to read. He is also the co-author of six *New York Times* bestsellers with well-known personalities, including *Use What You've Got* (with Shark Tank mogul Barbara Corcoran), *My Two Moms* (with civil rights advocate Zach Wahls), and *The Sell* (with Bravo star Fredrik Eklund).

Follow him **@brucelittlefield** and visit **www.brucelittlefield.com.**

Printed in the USA
CPSIA information can be obtained
at www.ICGtesting.com
LVHW060853260124
769861LV00026B/561/J